German Raiders
of the
South Seas

GERMAN RAIDERS
OF THE
SOUTH SEAS

The extraordinary truc story
of naval deception,
daring and disguise
1914–1917

ROBIN BROMBY

Highgate Publishing

German Raiders of the South Seas
First published 1985 Doubleday Australia

This expanded and revised edition published 2013

Highgate Publishing
P O Box 481
Edgecliff NSW 2027
Australia

National Library of Australia Cataloguing-in-Publication entry

Author: Bromby, Robin, 1942-
Title: German raiders of the South Seas [electronic resource]: the
extraordinary true story of naval deception, daring and
disguise 1914-1917 / Robin Bromby.

Edition: 2nd ed.
ISBN: 9780987403803 (ebook)
       9780987403810 (pbk)

Notes: Includes bibliographical references.
Subjects: Germany. Kriegsmarine.
World War, 1914-1918--Naval operations, German.
World War, 1914-1918--Pacific Ocean.

Dewey Number: 940.45943

Cover: Count Felix von Luckner

Contents

Prologue – The Raider

IN 1914 THE IDEA OF USING AN OSTENSIBLY innocent looking merchant vessel as a ship of war was not new. During the American Civil War a number of ships were built in Europe as fighting vessels for both sides. These were designed along the lines of merchantmen so that they could reach the side for which they were built in safety and, subsequently, operate as raiders. The Germans considered their use in 1870. Then in 1877 the Russian Government bought three steamers as the basis for its Russian Volunteer Fleet (one of whose ships features in this book) which would operate as merchantmen in peacetime. These were to be armed during hostilities and join regular naval units. Toward the end of the century German and British shipping companies, particularly the White Star Line, designed their vessels with provision for gun mountings, should these be needed. Several British and German ships had especially strengthened decks in anticipation of the need for armaments.

The first of the modern auxiliary cruisers was pressed into service by the Russians in their war against Japan in 1904, and their opponents quickly followed suit. By this time the Germans had already carried out tests on merchant ships and the Imperial Navy had taken over vessels for trials in order to judge how quickly a conversion could take place. A long list was soon compiled, covering the minimum speed requirements of new ships, radio equipment, tall masts and much more. The British were well aware of the danger, and even before war began a number of British ships carrying food from Australia and New Zealand had been equipped with stern guns.

The purpose of the surface raider was quite precise. No one had any illusions that they could stand and face a regular naval unit. Their purpose, rather, was to paralyse the enemy's sea trade. In the case of World War I, Britain was critically reliant on supplies from its empire to sustain the war effort. The U-boat could — and did — wreak havoc in the North Atlantic, but the farther reaches of the British Empire were beyond the range of submarines operating out of German ports. The surface raider could be more easily provisioned, and before the start of war could — unlike a U-boat or regular naval ship — position itself in foreign waters without raising suspicions. But once the hostilities began, the surface raiders could engender sufficient fear by their very presence so that the Allied navies had to commit ships (which were needed desperately elsewhere) to their pursuit.

This is the story of Germany's attempts to cut off Britain's supplies from its colonies and Dominions in the Pacific and Indian Oceans, particularly from Australia and New Zealand. One of the ships, the *Emden*, was not strictly an auxiliary cruiser, being a regular Imperial Navy fighting ship, but her operations were exactly that of the surface raider. Her captain and crew, like that of the *Wolf* which followed, displayed the highest standards of seamanship and tactical warfare and consequently inflicted heavy damage on Allied shipping. Had other raiders not suffered serious reverses, and the *Prinz Eitel Friedrich* and the *Cormoran* failed to find fuel and had the *Seeadler* not been wrecked, the raiders might have inflicted much greater losses in the seas around Australia and New Zealand.

As it was, they did quite enough.

1

The War Begins

ON 31 JULY 1914 as the shadows of war rolled in, the German cruiser *SMS Emden* slipped its moorings at the port of Tsingtao in northern China. The previous day had seen Austria-Hungary declare war on Serbia following the murder of Archduke Franz Ferdinand. Germany followed with declarations against France and Russia, and Britain and its empire would join in on 4 August.

Emden's captain, Karl von Müller, was anxious to avoid being bottled up in the harbour by the British naval squadron should war be declared. The Royal Navy was based not far away at Weihaiwei — the British territory on the North China coast which had been leased in 1898 for a coaling station (and would be returned to China in 1930). Although the Germans in China were aware that war was threatening, the timing of its declaration seems to have caught them by surprise; the main force of the East Asiatic Squadron was away on a three-month cruise of the Pacific to show the flag along the impressive string of German territories that spread as far as Samoa.

In 1884, the Emperor had proclaimed his sovereignty over the northern part of New Guinea. In 1897 the murder of two German missionaries in China had provided the pretext for the Germans to seize Kiaochow and extract a ninety-nine year lease on the bay at Tsingtao along with extensive railway and mining concessions in Shantung province from the beleaguered Chinese government. Kiaochow, while a German colony, was administered by the Reichsmarineamt and the governor of the territory was not a ministry official from Berlin but the commanding naval officer. Following the murder of the missionaries, Germany had sent a naval force and forced the weak Chinese government to accede to a 99-year lease on the territory; moreover, Germany was given the right to construct two railway lines into Chinese territory and have the rights to any minerals over a 30km-wide corridor through which those lines would run. The German victory set off another round of territorial claims for pieces of China: the Russians took over Port Arthur, France demand Kwangchow and Britain both expanded its land area at Hong Kong with a 99-year lease over what would be known as the New Territories and also took control at Weihaiwei in the north of China.

Meanwhile, in 1899 the Germans bought Marshall and Caroline Islands (now separately the countries of Palau and Federated States of Micronesia) from Spain and then Western Samoa was wrung from the British to complete the new and what would be a short-lived German empire in the east.

Nevertheless, the imperatives of the European situation were such that Germany could give only scant attention to its Pacific possessions. This may explain why the German fleet was scattered at the beginning of August. The armoured cruisers *Scharnhorst* and *Gneisenau*, each of 11,832 tons and launched in 1907 and 1908 respectively, were on the flag-showing cruise and the *Emden* was in Tsingtao, along with the armed merchant cruiser *Prinz Eitel Friedrich* and several colliers. The light cruiser *Nurnberg* was steaming from North America and due to meet up with *Scharnhorst* and *Gneisenau* at Apia in Samoa, while the other light cruiser, *Leipzig*, was en route to Mexico.

When the Nürnberg *was ordered to rejoin the East Asiatic Squadron at the outbreak of war, one of her first jobs was to cut the cable at Fanning Island, a relay station for the vital Pacific cable. On 7 September 1914 the cruiser landed a party of sailors, the Germans smashing the operating room, dynamiting the generating plant, dredging up the cable and cutting it.* [Paul Schmalenbach Collection]

Impressive though it was, Germany's naval squadron in the Pacific was dwarfed in size there by the country's merchant fleet operating in that vast ocean. At this time, Germany was second only to Britain in merchant tonnage there. In the Pacific the presence of the German territories as well as the normal international trade meant that German merchant ships were frequent visitors to British empire ports; many of the supplies needed by the German settlers in New Guinea came from Australia, and it was the German shipping companies which provided the transport for those supplies. The merchant ships, at least those with radios, could keep in contact with Berlin. In the early years of the twentieth century the Germans installed a network of wireless stations to link their possessions and their ships, the main stations being at Yap, New Guinea and Samoa. In 1908 all German merchant captains had received instructions that in time of war they were to head immediately for a German possession or a neutral port. In February 1914 all German ships equipped with wireless were told to listen to German stations at 0700, 1300 and 2310 each day.

On 3 August 1914, literally the eve of war, there were many German merchant ships around the coast of Australia. The *Seydlitz*, a Norddeutscher-Lloyd (NDL) mail steamer, was berthed at Sydney's Circular Quay. Also in Sydney that night were other NDL steamers: the *Elsass* at what was then the NDL wharf, the Melbourne at Garden Island and the *Osnabruck* at Woolloomooloo. The *Sumatra* had arrived from Hamburg the previous day, while the *Germania* was just in from the Caroline Islands. The *Stolberg* was docked at Fremantle and the *Scharzfels* and the *Iserlohn* had berthed at Adelaide, with the *Cannstadt* tieing up at Brisbane. The *Pommern* was at sea between Brisbane and Sydney.

From 3 August the Port of Sydney was closed at night. Three minutes after midnight on the previous day, at the other main port in New South Wales, Newcastle, the collier *Luneberg* had slipped out of that harbour with empty holds while the captain on the *Ulm* was so anxious to leave Newcastle he left two-thirds of his cargo on the wharf. The Australian authorities had already instructed the Navy to examine all ships entering or leaving defended ports.

The Seydlitz, *which escaped from Sydney Harbour on the eve of war and then sailed to Chile. There she joined the German East Asiatic Squadron. After escaping again — this time from the Battle of the Falklands which saw the German naval squadron largely destroyed —* Seydlitz *ended up being interned.* [Hapag-Lloyd AG]

On the evening of 3 August, the *Seydlitz* surprised Sydney port authorities by suddenly sliding away from her berth and turning down the harbour toward the heads. She was intercepted by customs agents at Bradley's Head, near the harbour entrance, but her papers were all correct and the ship was granted clearance. Originally, the *Seydlitz* had been due to sail for Bremen via Melbourne, Adelaide and Fremantle; her actual voyage was far more eventful. The ship was last seen heading south-east from Sydney ostensibly bound for Antwerp via Cape Horn (the Panama Canal was not to open for another two weeks). The *Seydlitz* made it safely to Chile where she was fully provisioned for the run home to Bremen which, when they learned of it, angered the

Royal Australian Navy. Instead of heading for Bremen, however, the ship joined the East Asiatic Squadron in time for the Battle of the Falklands. She followed the warships through the heavy seas south of Cape Horn. Luck was on her side. The Germans lost five cruisers and the two other supply ships in the battle with the Royal Navy off the Falklands; the *Seydlitz*, however, turned away under cover of darkness and sailed intact into the Argentine port of Bahia Blanca. She was there interned. (The Falklands engagement will be recounted in a later chapter.)

Back in Sydney another NDL ship had decided to follow the example of the *Seydlitz*: the *Elsass* put to sea so hurriedly, that in turning out of Woolloomooloo Bay, she smashed into the men's municipal baths at the edge of the Domain; the bow of the ship actually penetrated the pool. At high tide she backed out and headed for open sea. After that episode, and with several German ships pulling out of Newcastle, the Australian Government instructed its customs officers not to clear any more German vessels. The *Elsass* was later interned in American Samoa.

The Elsass, *another last minute escapee from Sydney, rammed the Woolloomooloo swimming baths as she made a dash for the open sea. She was interned at Pago Pago, American Samoa. Some of her crew would later join Count von Luckner in his breakout from a prisoner of war camp near Auckland.* [Hapag-Lloyd AG]

Several of the German merchantmen left their bids for freedom too late. By the time Australia was officially at war on 5 August (Australian time), the *Pfalz* had pulled away from Victoria Dock in Melbourne and was trying to make its escape. She passed Williamstown at full speed, but was stopped by a shot across the bows from Queenscliff Fort. The *Oberhausen* was seized at Port Huon in Tasmania while the *Greifswald* had sailed into Fremantle and captivity, her master unaware that the war had begun.

*   *   *

If the Germans seemed confused, then so too were the Australians. The country was in the middle of an election campaign called because Labor senators were frustrating the will of the Liberal majority in the House of Representatives. Federal parliament was still located in Melbourne at that time. On 31 July a telegram had arrived at Ballarat in Victoria addressed to Prime Minister Joseph Cook who the previous evening had spoken at an election meeting in the town. The telegram was from the Governor-General, Sir Ronald Munro-Ferguson, suggesting the cabinet should meet to decide what help it would give Britain in the event of war. Cook did not have the official cipher with him and was unable to read the message until the next day. A cabinet meeting was called for 3 August. Even so, this was not enough notice. Half of the ten-member cabinet was unable to attend the meeting, four being in far-flung corners of the country while the Postmaster General, Agar Wynne, was aboard ship heading for a postal conference in Madrid. Nevertheless, the five ministers at the meeting did not hesitate for a second to decide that Australia's place was at Britain's side. The Governor-General cabled the Secretary of State for the Colonies, Lewis Harcourt, that 'there is indescribable enthusiasm and entire unanimity throughout Australia in support of all that tends to provide for the security of the Empire in war'.

There was no less enthusiasm among the 1.14 million inhabitants of New Zealand. That country sent 100,000 men to fight for the Empire, of which one-sixth were killed. Total casualties, including wounded, amounted to 58,000 — almost five per cent of the entire population. Not even Belgium, the primary battleground of the western front, could match those casualty figures among its fighting forces. In Wellington, the New Zealand government had been worried its coastal towns or the coal reserves at Westport would come under bombardment from the German warships in the Pacific.

On 4 August the Admiralty in London had sent orders to all parts of the Empire that German colliers were to be detained. A state of war between Britain and Germany had been in existence for an hour before the news was received in Australia and New Zealand. The Australian official war history concluded that, while German shipping companies had been given advance warning from their head offices, most agents in Australia had to rely solely upon newspapers for information. The history quotes a telegram from the Sydney agent of the German-Australian Steamship Company to its headquarters in Hamburg on 1 August 1914 informing them that orders had been given to ships to sail, in one case, to Portuguese East Africa (which bordered German East Africa, now Tanzania) and, in the other, to the neutral Dutch East Indies:

> Have ordered *Essen* to Delagoa Bay; *Luneberg* leaves Newcastle this evening by direct route to Makassar in conformity with your instructions ... Is the instruction to *Ulm* valid for immediate departure?

The same day, Norddeutscher-Lloyd told its Sydney agent to discontinue freight and passenger bookings. It was all very last minute advice. The German government would not have sacrificed its large merchant fleet willingly; but whether this happened as a result of an oversight or wishful thinking is a matter for speculation.

Apart from the German vessels which were already in Australian ports, another thirteen were to sail into capture in the weeks which followed the outbreak of hostilities, the last being a sailing ship which arrived more than three months after the beginning of the war. One of the trapped steamers carried the official radio cipher which was immediately seized and used to effect by the Australians in decoding wireless messages for several months until a new code was substituted.

By the same token, the British steamer *Southport* had arrived in the Caroline Islands in September 1914, the captain obviously unaware that the war had begun. His ship was disabled by the Germans.

But, in that first few days of August when the Australian authorities began to tighten security, the residents of the German colonies were bracing themselves for an uncertain future. The 24-year-old Austro-Hungarian Franz Joseph I-class cruiser *Kaiserin Elisabeth* arrived at Tsingtao on 22 July seeking refuge. She was followed by a string of German vessels, all seeking the illusory security of this model German colony. *Kaiserin Elisabeth* was far too antiquated and slow to be reckoned as a force in the balance of naval power in the Pacific, and her crew was ordered to disarm the ship and travel overland to Tientsin. She was later scuttled after the Japanese had besieged and taken control of Tsingtao.

The electrifying news that Archduke Franz Ferdinand had been assassinated at Sarajevo in Bosnia on 28 June reached Tsingtao while the German fleet was away on its cruise. Von Müller of the

Emden was now the most senior naval officer at the Tsingtao base. He was eating dinner at the Prinz Heinrich Hotel when the news reached him and, soon after, German residents began to arrive, where they saw out the night drinking beer and singing patriotic German songs. Von Müller slipped away from the crowd to return to his ship. He gave orders for all non-essential equipment to be stripped from the *Emden*, particularly woodwork, furniture and curtains which could easily catch fire if the ship were to see action. The crew, which included Prince Franz Joseph of Hohenzollern, was pressed into action. The preparations on the ship were interrupted only by forays in the following days into the Yellow Sea for target practice.

The Emden *seen here at Tsingtao with a collier in the foreground.*
[Paul Schmalenbach Collection]

The *Emden* had been built in Danzig and launched in 1908. It was a small unarmoured cruiser, designed to intercept merchant shipping, particularly that of Britain. One of the ship's officers, Lieutenant Julius Lauterbach, recalled that when the *Emden* steamed out of Tsingtao on 31 July the crew felt alone against the world. Lauterbach, a self-styled sea dog and a reserve officer on active service, had spent many years in the China seas and he knew that easy pickings were to be found among the Russian mail steamers which plied between the Chinese ports and Vladivostok at the eastern terminus of the Trans-Siberian Railway.

Von Müller, by contrast with Lauterbach, was a cautious captain; he had sent a torpedo boat out of Tsingtao harbour to make certain that no foreign naval vessels were in the vicinity. Once at sea the crew of the *Emden* was promptly put on action stations to keep them alert. Over the previous few days the ship's officers had debated what they should do. The German declaration of war on Russia resolved that discussion.

On 4 August 1914, the day upon which the last fateful act was being played out in the chancelleries of London, Paris and Berlin, the *Emden* sighted the first of its victims — the Russian mail steamer *Rjasan*, built in Germany in 1909 and capable of fourteen knots. Several Japanese ships had already been sighted by the Germans but Japan was still dithering about its entry into the war (and did not join the Allies until later that month). As the *Emden* headed north von Müller had his mind on the Russian naval base at Vladivostok. He knew that the Royal Navy would soon be the primary foe in the China seas, but the declaration of war with Britain had not reached him and so the Russians would have to suffice in the meantime.

According to an account given in 1917 by the German cruiser's second-in-command, Kapitanleutnant Hellmuth von Mücke, 'with decks cleared for action and lights out, the Emden proceeded through the Straits of Tsushima at fifteen knots on a black and moonless night'. The Germans, as well as Russian and British ships, also had the French to avoid: they knew that somewhere in the northern China seas a squadron consisting of the armoured cruisers *Montcalm* and *Dupleix*, along with several destroyers, was patrolling.

It was then that the *Rjasan* was spotted, just an outline in the night sky. No lights, no colours. The Russians saw the *Emden* at the same time and turned abruptly to head for neutral Japanese waters. As the dawn light came up the *Emden* was close enough to fire a blank shell across the Russian's bow but that did not stop her. Von Müller ordered two more shots to be aimed high: the salvoes crashed out from the forward battery, shells screamed over the *Rjasan*'s stacks and landed in the water ahead of her. She hove to and a boarding party was dispatched from the German ship. Lauterbach headed the prize crew and found the Russian captain to be an old acquaintance. The captain said he did not speak German. 'Well', he said according to a later account by Lauterbach, 'you have forgotten a lot. You knew German well enough fourteen days ago when we were drinking beer together at the club in Tsingtao'. That broke the ice. The *Rjasan* put about for Tsingtao, the first German naval prize of the war.

The Rjasan, *a Russian mail steamer caught by the* Emden. *It was commissioned by the Germans as* Cormoran *to replace the naval vessel of that name which was still undergoing a refit at Tsingtao.* [Paul Schmalenbach Collection]

The new prize was a timely opportunity for the crews of the small ships stranded at Tsingtao. Apart from the East Asiatic Squadron, the Germans had maintained a small fleet to keep peace and show the flag around the islands of the South Pacific, and to patrol the Chinese rivers. This fleet included the survey ship *Planet* (which was at Yap in the Carolines at this time) and two gunboats of considerable vintage. One of these gunboats had already finished her tour of duty and was on her way back to Germany. The other, the *Cormoran*, had been in dry dock at Tsingtao undergoing a refit (and would also later be scuttled along with the Austrian cruiser). This refit, incidentally, involved the dismantling of the ship's engines, which supports the claim that the Germans in China were taken by surprise by the timing of war. This is even further borne out by the fact that just two months previously, the commander of the British China Squadron itself, Vice-Admiral Sir Martyn Jerram, had paid a courtesy call at Tsingtao.

Cormoran's crew, enjoying a long shore leave, had been joined by the crews of the Yangtze River gunboats *Otter*, *Vaterland* and *Tsingtao* who had been instructed in July to disarm and abandon their vessels and travel overland to the German colony.

The capture of the *Rjasan* solved the problem for the Germans of what to do with these surplus crews. The commander of the disabled *Cormoran*, Korvettenkapitan Adalbert Zuckschwerdt, had decided in von Müller's absence to mount guns on the luxury liner *Prinz Eitel Friedrich* and man the ship with some of his surplus sailors. Now, with the *Emden's* prize, he had two auxiliary cruisers at his disposal.

The *Rjasan* had been a member of the Russian Volunteer Fleet and had clearly been designed to be converted to an auxiliary cruiser. Von Müller decided she could well fit this role in the cause of Imperial Germany, with Zuckschwerdt and his men to be her crew. The former Russian ship was moored alongside the disabled *Cormoran*. The first task was to clean her up, Russian standards of cleanliness at sea being far removed from Teutonic hygiene requirements. On shore, meanwhile, frantic preparations were being made for the defence of Tsingtao itself. The harbour was mined and gun emplacements set up along the waterfront. Small ships were being loaded ready to act as colliers to the German fleet.

Within two days they had the *Rjasan* ready to sail. She was now re-named *Cormoran* in place of the shell of a ship still lying at the dock. The main problem for Zuckschwerdt was fuel capacity. The question of coaling the surface raiders is a recurring one throughout this book: not only were commanders constantly concerned where the next supply of coal was coming from, but, when coal was available, getting it aboard ship was a backbreaking and filthy job. Away from ports there was inevitably no crane to help, only the crew working with shovels and buckets. Raiders of World War I, while charged with sinking Allied shipping in order to starve Britain of supplies, eyed many possible victims with the single thought of how much coal they might be carrying. As will be seen later, German colonies were justified in Berlin on the sole grounds of their potential as coaling stations for the Imperial Navy.

In the case of the newly re-named *Cormoran* the solution to the problem of limited fuel capacity was to move the crew on to the deck and use the ship's accommodation as extra coal bunkers. By this means Zuckschwerdt gave his ship an additional 16,000 kilometre range. He sailed out of Tsingtao on 10 August 1914. Four months later he and his crew were to be interned by the Americans at Guam, but a great deal would happen to the *Cormoran* before then.

Meanwhile the might of the British Empire was preparing to expel Germany once and for all from the Pacific. She had not been wanted there in the first place. To the British and Germans the Pacific was a sideshow at a time of momentous events on the European continent. Indeed, many histories of World War I scarcely mention the events taking place so far away from London, Paris, Berlin and St Petersburg. The Germans and the British knew that the question of naval supremacy would be settled in the North Sea and the Atlantic Ocean. The wider questions of strategy and planning will be dealt with in the next chapter, but it is clear from contemporary accounts that the people of Australia and New Zealand had a considerable fear of a German presence in the Pacific Ocean. There had been a number of Russian 'scares' in the late nineteenth century and, particularly in New Zealand, defensive installations had been undertaken at some harbours in anticipation of the Tsar's warships suddenly appearing on the horizon. Australia was not quite so hysterical: in 1909 the Australian government noted that the term 'defended port' was an empty one, those ports so designated (Sydney, Adelaide, Newcastle, Port Phillip, for example) either had no guns, or if they did, had no trained gunnery officers, searchlights for night firing or supplies for the crews.

But by the outbreak of war, the scare was really on in both countries. On 10 August, the *New Zealand Herald* reported the Australians were worried about 'the great naval base of Simpsonhafen (now Rabaul) in Kaiser Wilhelm land (now part of Papua New Guinea) which had allegedly been built at a cost of 'thousands of pounds'. The newspaper which, despite hostilities, was still printing daily summaries of local shipping movements, warned that the German naval base had been built under the guise of mercantile expansion within striking distance of the Torres Strait, where all the shipping routes between Australia and the Far East converged. It reported that the wharf at Simpsonhafen was

300 metres long with spacious warehouses worth £40,000; if these had existed, this imaginary wharf would have been longer than any other in Australasia and equal to the needs of a city of 100,000 people. The report of this 'great naval base' would have been news to the Imperial German Navy, too.

At the outbreak of war, the East Asiatic Squadron faced a superior British and Allied presence and the squadron commander, Vice-Admiral Maximilian Count von Spee, knew that only too well. Apart from the Russian fleet at Vladivostok and the two French cruisers, *Dupleix* and *Montcalm*, there was the British China squadron based at Weihaiwei and Hong Kong, the East Indies station at Colombo, and the Australian squadron.

It was a great day when HMAS Australia *led the new Australian fleet into Sydney. The power of this ship alone was sufficient to make von Spee keep well clear of it — it was the one ship the Germans knew could blow them out of the water.* [Australian War Memorial]

Britain's China fleet had the cruiser *Minotaur* as its flagship, the cruiser *Hampshire*, the pre-Dreadnought battleship *Triumph*, the light cruisers *Newcastle* and *Yarmouth* and the destroyers *Chelmer*, *Colne* and *Fame*. The East Indies squadron included the slow battleship Swiftsure, and the light cruisers *Dartmouth* and *Fox*. In terms of firepower, the bigger British ships were a match for the German cruisers; but they could not manage the latter's speed.

One ship that could, however, was the pride of the new Australian navy established only three years previously, the battle cruiser *Australia* (19,580 tons, launched 1912). A post-war account described her as 'one of the best naval vessels in the Pacific'. The recently-built *Australia* could outshoot any of the opposing German ships. Von Spee was preoccupied above all else with avoiding that vessel. The Australians also had the light cruisers *Melbourne* and *Sydney* (the *Brisbane* was under construction), the light cruiser *Encounter* on loan from the Admiralty, the destroyers *Parramatta*, *Yarra* and *Warrego*, and two submarines. The squadron had steamed into Sydney Harbour for the first time on 4 October 1913, commanded by Rear Admiral Sir George Patey. The fleet was greeted on that day by huge crowds lining Farm Cove, and a fervent outburst of patriotism (and jingoism) by both public and politicians alike. The *Sydney Morning Herald* reported Prime Minister Joseph Cook telling the welcoming banquet that

> our self-respect requires the building of this fleet ... that these huge preparative expenditures are better than being bled white and humiliated ... These boats are being built simply to maintain a freedom for which our Empire is famous, to guard the justice on which it stands, the opportunities which it promotes, the hopes that it inspires, the pieties it enshrines, the literature it possesses and the organising ability it begets.

In a word, we have to begin this building of our fleet because we ought to, and we must.

Over the Tasman Sea in New Zealand the Royal Navy had stationed the cruiser *Philomel* (which could make nineteen knots 'if pressed') and the third class cruisers *Psyche* and *Pyramus*, a class of ship described as 'unspeakably useless' by the First Naval Member of the Australian Naval Board, Rear-Admiral Sir William Creswell. At the other end of the Pacific the Japanese, who had been more than ever convinced of the efficacy of naval power after sinking the Russian Baltic Fleet in 1905 at the Battle of Tsushima Straits, possessed a considerable fleet of battleships and battle-cruisers, armoured and light cruisers. She was not yet in the war, but von Spee knew that Japan was tied to Britain by a treaty, and that its navy was to be reckoned with.

New Zealand's main protector, the ancient Philomel *which could make 19 knots 'if pressed'.* [Royal New Zealand Navy]

The Pyramus, *the third class cruiser sent by Britain to reassure the*
New Zealanders they were being defended. An Australian admiral described
this class as being 'unspeakably useless'. [Royal New Zealand Navy]

In the last week of July 1914, and the last week of peace, the Royal Australian Navy was on its winter cruise off the coast of Queensland, the balance of its fleet lying at Sydney and Port Phillip. As the official war history notes, 'a more placid situation could scarcely be conceived'. It was not until 10.30 pm on the evening of 30 July that the fleet was recalled to Sydney to prepare for war.

By 5 August, it was back at sea. The Australians were looking for German naval ships and were keeping a constant listening watch on the German radio station at Yap, the most powerful in the enemy's wireless network. One Australian listening post received a distinct message instructing the *Scharnhorst* to go to he Marianas Islands but this was disregarded, perhaps because it was thought to be a trick (not that it mattered — there was an inexplicable ten-day delay between the message being intercepted by the Australians and its being read by naval command).

Admiral Patey was aboard the *Australia*. He preferred the theory that the German fleet under von Spee was at Simpsonhafen in New Guinea. By the afternoon of 11 August the Australians were off the German harbour, braced for action, and the *Warrego* actually went alongside the jetty. Apparently this visit was not noticed by the Germans, and the Australians found nothing of interest to them. Next morning the ships returned to Herbertshohe, the main German port in New Guinea, to look for the wireless station. A landing party quizzed some German residents who refused to help. The ships then began to move along the coast while the lookouts scanned the shore and hills for any tell-tale wireless masts. Operators aboard the Australian ships heard the elusive station sending out a message that six enemy ships were lying off Rabaul. In the meantime, members of the *Warrego*'s crew went ashore at Rabaul to wreck the post office. But von Spee was not to be found.

It was not until September that the Australians had the chance to bag an important German ship — which they missed so doing due to the most extraordinary of circumstances. The replacement *Cormoran* and the *Prinz Eitel Friedrich* had met von Spee in the Carolines, and then been dispatched to raid shipping off the coast of Western Australia. As the colliers designated to replenish the fuel supplies of the two raiders had not appeared, Zuckschwedt decided to look for colliers in New Guinea waters and raid the eastern coast of Australia instead. He reached the coast of mainland New Guinea on 24 September and sought shelter in Port Grand

Duke Alexis. By a stunning coincidence, just twenty kilometres away the Australians were that very day occupying Wilhelmshafen, the seat of the German administration on mainland New Guinea.

Two days later the *Cormoran's* lookouts reported the approach of four ships. These turned out to be the *Australia* and the *Encounter*, the French cruiser *Montcalm* and the Australian armed merchant cruiser *Berrima*. The German raider was anchored in one of the small bays behind small coral reefs and the overhanging jungle. While the German crew held their breath, the *Encounter* and the *Berrima* moved into Port Alexis while the two Australian larger ships remained out to sea. Slowly, as the Australian ships circled the harbour, Zuckschwerdt was turning his vessel so that all his guns came to bear on the Australians.

The Australian cruiser Encounter — *which failed to live up to her name when she passed within metres of, and did not detect, the German raider* Cormoran. Encounter *was a Royal Navy cruiser on loan to Australia until* HMAS Brisbane *was completed. She stayed on in Australia after the war as a training ship.* [Australian War Memorial 300621]

Astoundingly, the Australian sailors aboard *Encounter* slid by within 100 metres of their quarry and saw nothing. When the Australian ships left the harbour, and made steam for departure, the Germans could hardly believe their luck. After an outpouring of emotional relief, Zuckschwerdt ordered a course back to Yap with the thought of returning and attacking the Australian troops which had landed in New Guinea. He took the crew of the survey ship *Planet* aboard, and left a small party behind to blow her up.

Zuchschwerdt's resolve soon evaporated: with every kilometre he had come closer to New Guinea, so the strength of wireless transmissions from the Australian ships kept increasing. He turned north again, eventually to surrender to internment in Guam. (*Prinz Eitel Friedrich* had failed to find the *Cormoran* at a New Guinea rendezvous, then raided off the Atlantic coast of South America, and eventually surrendered at Newport News in the United States.)

The problem facing all the German ships was that their wireless stations had gradually been captured by the Australians and New Zealanders, making it impossible for them to locate any German colliers still in the region. The wireless station in New Guinea had been operating for only a month before the war had begun. The station was erected about fifteen kilometres inland, and in late July the Berlin company building the station had erected a temporary mast so the station could begin operating ahead of schedule. This station, and the one at Apia, were operating just in time to hear the news that they were at war. The Germans on Samoa had already started to wonder: von Spee's squadron had been due to visit Apia on 27 July and considerable organisation had gone into the welcome celebrations. The failure of the ships to appear off Apia that day had been a great disappointment to the community.

Von Spee had been more concerned with saving his ships. He was not going to provide the British with a sitting target (and he was to learn on 27 August that Japan was in the war, too). At the beginning of August, he had been at Pagan in the Marianas Islands when his tour of the Pacific was interrupted. He had the *Scharnhorst* and the *Gneisenau* and the collier *Titania* with him. He immediately ordered the *Nurnberg* to meet him there instead of in Samoa, and the rest of his fleet to make for that point as quickly as they could. Von Spee was aware of his ability to create havoc amongst British and Empire shipping, but it seems unlikely that he fully appreciated the degree to which uncertainty of his whereabouts in those early days had caused great consternation among British forces. No one was sure where he would turn up, which led to the delay in the departure of Australian and New Zealand troopships across the Indian Ocean for the trenches in France.

Von Spee was just as anxious to avoid the British. The *Emden* had got away from Tsingtao in time to avoid being hemmed in by the British cruisers. Their commander, Vice-Admiral Jerram, wanted to marshal several of his ships off Weihaiwei which would have given him a good chance of coming across the *Emden* as it sailed north, while he ordered the *Yarmouth* to sail north from Shanghai to seal off that line of escape and effectively close the door on the Yellow Sea. He did not, however, figure on the Admiralty in London: they countermanded Jerram and told him to assemble his squadron off Hong Kong, nearly 1,500 kilometres away. It was one of the more costly naval blunders of the war. Before the Allies caught up with her again, the *Emden* would have sunk eighteen ships.

Von Müller, having thus eluded the British, met von Spee at Pagan. There he put his case for the *Emden* to be detached from the rest of the squadron, and for him to be left with a free hand to raid enemy shipping. Von Spee agreed, and assigned von Müller the collier *Markomannia*.

Soon the name *Emden* would be known around the world.

2

Germany's imperial dream

IN 1900 Admiral Alfred von Tirpitz, State Secretary of the German Imperial Naval Board, took a bill to the Reichstag. Not only did that piece of legislation signal Germany's intention to achieve parity with the Royal Navy in the North Sea and Atlantic, it also provided for a distant waters fleet of three heavy, and twenty-four light, cruisers.

One significant problem facing the German Navy was the lack of coal and coaling stations to serve those ships once they had been commissioned. For example, the cruiser *Dresden* required 170 tons of coal every twenty-four hours in order to maintain a speed of twenty knots. Her total bunker capacity was 850 tons. This rate of consumption could be reduced by lower speeds, and some of the surface raiders frequently kept speed down to four or five knots between periods of action in order to conserve coal, but it was still necessary to have readily available re-coaling ports. To this end, the German navy set out to establish *etappendienst*, or staging posts, at various points around the world, backed up by orders to all German merchantmen that they must always be ready to take coal and other supplies to warships.

German colonies were the most secure form of *etappendienst* and, in times of conflict, sanctuary for German ships. But colonies were attractive for one other important reason. Germany needed new markets if it was to combat unemployment at home. Emigration was a major concern: between 1871 and 1881, some 800,000 people left the newly united Germany; taking the period 1887 to 1906, the figure grows to over one million. But here was the rub for Germany: almost all of those emigrants went to the United States. By contrast, while many British went to America, large numbers also chose Canada, New Zealand, South Africa and Australia; in other words, Britain 'kept' the bulk of its emigrants within its empire, thereby enlarging its own export markets and simultaneously increasing the strength of that Empire. For the Germans, by contrast, their emigrants were lost forever.

Chancellor Bismarck had previously frustrated the colonial lobby simply because he did not want to antagonise Britain or France; anyway, colonies were not part of his design for Germany's future. In 1884, however, he did a volte-face and approved the annexation of five territories: New Guinea (including New Britain, New Ireland and part of the Solomon Islands), South-West Africa, Togoland, the Cameroons and Tanganyika. The Germans were now convinced territories — and a fleet to protect their trade lines — had become a necessity. The phobia that Britain and other foreign competitors would try to destroy that trade was accentuated by ever-increasing German unemployment in the last decades of the century.

But then, as economic conditions improved after 1900, emigration from Germany slowed to a trickle. Moreover, getting immigrants interested in the new German colonies was not easy:

there were no temperate ones with large swathes of potential farmland, or anything vaguely approaching the appeal of the Cape Colony, New Zealand, Canada or the Australian colonies. The Cameroons and Togoland were seen as tropical hellholes, and South-West Africa was unsuited to farming because so much of it was arid. By 1913, this entire empire was home to just 23,500 Germans, and many of those were serving in the administrations, army or police forces rather than as people making a new home. This lack of critical mass of Europeans in the German colonies also meant these territories never became a meaningful market for manufactured goods from the home country.

The Australian colonies also had their eyes on New Guinea. The Dutch had already taken the western half of the island. New Guinea was separated from the mainland of Australia only by the narrow Torres Strait, and the Queenslanders and others had no desire to see a foreign and potentially unfriendly power ensconced just across that narrow waterway.

There was already a considerable German presence in New Guinea. The Germans had acquired labourers for their plantations in Samoa from the Melanesian tribes, and pressure was being brought to bear within Germany to secure this valuable source of cheap manpower by annexation.

Interest in the island from the Australian colonies was growing. The forceful Queensland premier, Sir Thomas McIlwraith, told the Colonial Office in London his government would meet the cost of governing New Guinea if only the British would cable him the authority to annex it. As it happened, the Queenslanders could not wait, especially once the news got out that a German ship had left Sydney on 18 March 1883. It was suspected that its mission was to claim New Guinea for the German Reich. On 4 April an agent of the Queensland Government, acting on

McIlwraith's orders, landed at Port Moresby to proclaim possession for the Crown of all of New Guinea east of the Dutch border. The governments of New South Wales, Victoria and South Australia quickly rushed to support McIlwraith, but on 2 July the British Government disavowed the annexation. Lord Derby, Secretary of State for the Colonies, privately supported the Queensland initiative but was not able to carry the cabinet. The Australians saw it as a case of Downing Street sleeping while the Germans laid the foundations of an empire.

The Germans took advantage of the dithering by the British, and raised their flag on the northern coast of New Guinea. The British Government, confronted by this development, was furious. Although not then in the government (but later to be colonial secretary himself), Joseph Chamberlain spoke for British public opinion when he said: 'I don't care about New Guinea, and I am not afraid of German colonisation, but I don't like to be cheeked by Bismarck or anyone else'. Britain promptly proclaimed its sovereignty over the southern part of the island, the territory to be known as Papua.

The Germans, meanwhile, had marked out their claim. Northeast mainland New Guinea became Kaiser Wilhelmsland, New Britain was renamed Neu Pommern, and New Ireland was now Neu Mecklenburg. The village of Kokopo, on Neu Pommern, was the main German administrative centre and was renamed Herbertshohe. But what scared the Australians more than changes of nomenclature was that Germany now had a potential naval base in their backyard (and in New Zealand's backyard once the Germans acquired the western islands of Samoa).

Where the flag went, so went German trading companies. The most famous was the Hamburg house of Godeffroy which had set up its first trading base in Samoa in 1857. In 1872 an

English visitor to the Gilbert and Ellice Islands reported that almost all the white men there were agents of a Godeffroy ally, Weber and Company of Apia. That same year a Royal Navy ship found a Godeffroy agent established at Ponape in the Caroline Islands. In fact, by the end of the 1870s the company had posts and agencies in Fiji, Tonga, the Solomon Islands, the New Hebrides, New Britain and the Marshall Islands as well. They were out to corner the copra trade. And they were supported back in Germany by an insistent new group, the *Kolonialverein,* which advocated the importance of trade with colonial territories.

German ships traded with non-German islands including Tonga. It was significant that German companies had established themselves in the region well before the imperial thrust from Berlin. Hermsheim Company opened a branch at Yap, part of the Caroline Islands, in 1873 to trade copra. In 1903, the Germans discovered phosphate on Angaur Island in the Carolines (now in the Republic of Palau) and in 1909 Deutsche Sudsee Phosphat AG began mining, production rising to 90,000 tons in 1913.

The aggressiveness of Godeffroy's trade is amply illustrated by the fact in the first three years of its agency in Apia, fourteen German ships called there compared to eleven British and thirteen American. The major trade in coconut oil was supplemented by pearl and tortoiseshell. By 1865 the company had developed the first commercial coconut plantation in Samoa and had planted 1,400 hectares with cotton. In 1879, however, the Godeffroy company collapsed, a failure primarily due to the German economic crisis which had begun in 1873 but also partly caused by its own speculative activities in Europe. This failure was seen as a blow to German prestige in the new empire. Bismarck tried to get the Reichstag to bail out the company but the parliamentarians would not support this, it being left to a group of banks to finance a new company to buy the Godeffroy assets. Bismarck did not want to lose Germany's toehold in the island group and was well aware that New Zealand had intentions to establish its own little empire in the South Pacific with Samoa near the top of the list.

The German companies were careful to chose well-educated, multilingual young men to staff their trading posts. They were also greatly assisted by the fact that, unlike the British or French, German shipping lines had established a fast direct service to Europe. The increasing availability of steamships made it possible for the Germans also to add fast shipping operations between the islands and Hong Kong and Sydney.

The overall success of the German-based companies was shown by their trading results. The Deutsche Handels-und Plantagen-Gesellschaft had increased its dividend from eight to thirty-six per cent between 1900 and 1914. The small Deutsche Neu-Guinea Kompagnie had expanded its capital to £375,000 pounds and bought a fleet of ships, much of the company's success coming from the New Guinea trade now free from British and Australian competition. In Neu Pommern, settlers were offered especially low rates for agreeing to ship only with a German line for a five-year contract period. The German companies controlled most of the auxiliary schooners operating between the smaller ports and which fed passengers and freight into their own ocean-going ships. The German Government gave these companies extremely generous mail contracts which by 1914 totalled 1.3 million marks a year. While they might have to compete for outward freight to Australia and New Zealand, the German companies also had a monopoly on the cartage of coal back to the islands from the British Dominions. Within a year of German annexation, these companies were exporting more than 2,000 tons of copra annually from Neu Pommern. Now it was time to turn their attention to other Territories.

In 1885 Germany tried to compete with the Spanish for the Caroline Islands but the Pope, to whom the dispute was referred, arbitrated in favour of Spain; although the Germans did extract the right to trade freely throughout the group, a concession which — given Spain's maritime inferiority — put Germany in a position where it had the economic advantage. A German naval captain hoisted his country's flag on the island of Jaluit in the Marshall group without provoking any protest, and in 1899 the Germans purchased the Carolines and Marianas to consolidate their foothold in Micronesia.

They had no such easy road in Samoa, despite the well established plantations owned by their companies. Tirpitz was arguing to his government that Samoa should be a coaling station for the Imperial Navy so that the East Asiatic Squadron could re-coal on its way from Tsingtao to South America. As a result of complex negotiations, Britain withdrew its claims in Western Samoa in exchange for the German Solomon Islands and other territories. On 1 March 1900 the Germans officially proclaimed their control at Apia. At the ceremony at which the flag was hoisted, Captain Emsmann of the original *Cormoran* told the assembled gathering that 'where the German eagle has stuck his talons into a land, the land is German and German shall remain'.

Tirpitz saw the colonies as a means whereby the prestige of the German navy could be enhanced, particularly with the Reichstag on which he depended for the money to build the German High Seas Fleet. So, at budget time, one of the documents which reached the Reichstag deputies was a lavish annual report on the development of Tsingtao. If nothing else, Tirpitz realised the acquisition of colonies throughout the Pacific Basin would, in itself, justify the need for more ships for their defence. In 1899 the German Navy League printed pamphlets which urged the acquisition of Samoa and construction of ships to guard it. The fact that Germany had to abandon other interests in order to acquire Samoa engendered bitter feeling against Britain at the time, feeling which was channelled into the campaign for a larger navy and an eventual reckoning with the British. In 1899 when the Germans dreaded that Samoa might slip from their grasp at the last moment, the *Kolnische Zeitung* newspaper noted that the situation had taught 'the German people the value and nature of a fleet … in order that Germany will not one day be crushed against the wall'. The hysteria gave Tirpitz the advantage needed to extract the money he sought for his fleet. The irony is that Tirpitz never seriously considered Apia as a base. Its harbour was too dangerous; a German navy vessel, *Adler,* had gone down on the reef at the harbour entrance with considerable loss of life in 1889. Samoa had served to rally support for a larger navy, a navy which Tirpitz intended to use at home against the British. Once he had his money, however, Samoa was of no further importance to him. It would be the raider rather than the regular navy that would wish there were more German havens in the Pacific.

The German East Asiatic Squadron at Apia —showing the flag. Apia was never seriously considered as a coaling base for the fleet due to its dangerous harbour entrance. [Paul Schmalenbach Collection]

The British, also, had little desire to become embroiled in protracted naval warfare in the Pacific. While Australia and New Zealand would in 1914 offer the flower of their youth to the British sacrificial altar along the Western Front, the Admiralty in London was almost totally preoccupied with the balance of sea power in the North Sea. When London did show concern about naval matters around the other side of the world, it was in response to a threat to the flow of supplies to Britain. The *Emden* became a particular nuisance when, through its successes in raids around the Indian Ocean, it interrupted the regular flow of troop transports carrying Empire regiments to the Western Front in France.

Sir John Fisher, who had become First Sea Lord in the early years of the century, felt which way the wind was blowing. He knew that the crucial problem was to equip a fleet to protect Britain's sea approaches. Yet, around the vast reaches of empire, the Royal Navy was dependent on a varied and antiquated fleet. Gunboats and small warships abounded, showing the flag but totally useless in battle. The advent of the dreadnoughts and the advances in naval armament meant the smaller ocean-going ships were too slow or were inadequately armed to be useful in any major naval engagement. Fisher told the Government in 1904 that, of the 193 commissioned ships at his disposal, all but sixty-three were next to useless. By a stroke of the pen he consigned many of the more obsolete ships to the scrap yard.

An essential part of his plan was to reduce the fleet in the farther seas, especially the Pacific. The Prince of Wales (later King George V) wrote to Fisher urging the retention of the ships then in the Pacific, but to no avail.

Where did this leave Australia and New Zealand? Nervous and apprehensive, to say the least. The Australasian Naval Agreement of 1887 provided that Australia and New Zealand would pay for the maintenance of Royal Navy ships in these waters. No one, by the turn of the century, was very happy with this arrangement. The British had their own naval problems and priorities, while the Australians, particularly, were more interested in building a separate Australian fleet. Growing disquiet at the dependence on Britain and the Royal Navy was further enhanced with the arrival of the American 'Great White Fleet' in 1908. The United States Atlantic Fleet caused a great commotion as it sailed into Sydney Harbour, drawing enormous crowds to the waterfront and giving rise to unprecedented celebrations.

The visit inspired the new Labor Government under Andrew Fisher to order, as one of its first acts, the planning for a fleet of destroyers. The matter became confused however, when New South Wales and Victoria offered to pay the cost of battleships for the Royal Navy. But in 1909 Australia was once more resolved to go ahead with its fleet. This was to consist of the battle-cruiser *Australia*, the cruisers *Brisbane, Sydney* and *Melbourne*, six destroyers and two submarines. Fortunately a large part of the force was to be completed by the outbreak of war.

The British, meanwhile, continued to withdraw ships from the region as the struggle with Germany for naval supremacy in the Atlantic and North Sea continued.

The New Zealanders were less keen to cut the apron strings. They did not feel they could defend themselves and, in retrospect, seem to have missed an opportunity to forge a common naval policy with Australia. After all, they were in the same part of the world and had similar interests in keeping belligerent powers out of the Pacific. However, on 22 March 1909 the New Zealand government of Sir Joseph Ward advised London it was willing to meet the cost of the immediate construction of a first class battle-ship and, if necessary, a second. The British gratefully accepted the offer and the New Zealand government was authorised by the Naval Defence Act of 1909 to borrow £2 million for the cost of a ship. The Admiralty could hardly avoid naming her *HMS New Zealand* and she was laid down in June 1910, launched in July the following year, and commissioned in November 1912. She displaced nearly 19,000 tons and was capable of twenty-six knots. The motivation in Wellington for this generosity had been the fear of German aggression in the Pacific, or the use of that country's warships against a vulnerable Dominion, and the New Zealanders were already alarmed by the number of potential German bases rather too close to their shores. The pact between Britain and Japan, while it might relieve the pressure on Britain in the East, was of little comfort. The 'Yellow Peril' scare was then at its zenith in the antipodes, and if anything, Japan was seen as just as great a threat as Germany.

Nearly a century on, and without taking into account the fact that New Zealanders then saw themselves as more or less part of Britain, the absurdity of the Dominion paying for the ship and then acceding to requests from the Admiralty to station *New Zealand* in the North Sea stands out starkly in hindsight, as does Wellington's agreement to take in exchange three quite palpably obsolete light cruisers. The British simply reneged on their undertakings to ensure security in the Pacific, and the New Zealanders swallowed what they were given. One of the few people who realised New Zealand was getting a raw deal was the Minister of Defence, James Allen, who wanted New Zealand to follow Australia's example in developing its own fleet. At least the people of New Zealand, who footed the bill, got to glimpse the *New Zealand* when she visited the country as part of a world cruise in 1913.

That same year at a conference in London, however, a plan for the establishment of the New Zealand Naval Forces was agreed to, which allowed that New Zealand should train her own men and the *Philomel* was loaned as a seagoing training ship. It was commissioned as a New Zealand ship in Wellington in July 1914. The Admiralty also agreed to station the light cruisers *Psyche* and *Pyramus* in New Zealand waters. (In 1921 a separate force was established but even then it was called the New Zealand Division of the Royal Navy.)

But at least the New Zealand ships had access to good coal. It was well established by 1914 that Australian coal was seriously defective for steaming purposes. Tests aboard *HMAS Australia* a few months before the war showed that, to keep the screws turning at 186 revolutions per minute for a specified period of time, sixteen tons of New South Wales coal was required against twelve and a half tons of New Zealand Westport coal or ten tons of Welsh coal. The Welsh coal would not be forthcoming in times of war, and at the outbreak of the war the Australian navy had only 1,800 tons of Westport coal in reserve. At the end of July there was practically no coal held in reserve at all. Fortunately, the Union Steam Ship Company, which was then owned by Britain's Peninsular and Orient company (but still maintained itself primarily as a New Zealand line), placed its colliers at the disposal of the defence effort and proceeded to deliver substantial quantities of Westport coal to the Royal Australian Navy, including to the depots at Port Moresby and Noumea.

The time had come to rid the Pacific of Germans.

3

Kicking out the Germans

German New Guinea native troops receiving instructions in musketry.
[Australian War Memorial A2545]

TWO DAYS AFTER THE declaration of war between Britain and Germany, the call went out from London to Australia and New Zealand. Australia was asked to seize the German wireless stations at Yap, Nauru and New Guinea, and New Zealand was asked to take care of Samoa (the Japanese would occupy the Caroline and Marshall Islands when they joined the war). Politicians in Melbourne, Wellington, and Whitehall were apprehensive about the succour the German colonies and their wireless stations could give the East Asiatic Squadron. The wireless and the coaling stations, had they not been captured by Allied forces, would have enabled von Spee to cruise at will throughout the Pacific.

In fact von Spee had no intention of hanging around the South Pacific, especially if there was any chance he would come into contact with the *Australia*. The Germans had auxiliary cruiser warfare on their minds. For many years German vessels had carefully charted the Pacific, particularly noting havens for their ships. The Germans had been particularly secretive about their wireless stations, not wanting to alert any potential enemy to the importance of the network; the station on Nauru, for example, had used a low-powered transmitter until the eve of war, and only then brought the main transmitter into service startling a military listening post in Melbourne with the sudden clarity and power of its signal.

There was no consistent policy from Berlin about defending the colonies in time of war. There was a force in Tanganyika which put up a fight until 1917, and German sailors resisted the Japanese during the attack on Tsingtao, but Samoa was surrendered without any resistance and opposition was short-lived in New Guinea. The islands of the scattered Caroline, Marshall and Marianas groups had few German residents let alone any troops. Samoa had a small militia, but that was mainly to ensure the natives kept the peace; a suggestion that a native force be raised to help defend the colony in case of external attack was rejected by the governor on the grounds that the Samoans could just as easily turn their weapons on their German masters.

Only in New Guinea was there any attempt to organise a defence. The governor there had decided a force should defend the wireless station at Bita Paka, inland from Herbertshohe, or the capital if that were attacked, but these forces could have provided only delaying action. The Germans had a number of army reservists who trained and commanded an expeditionary force of 125 native troops, while the Colonial Office in Berlin supplied a regular army officer for the force. On 6 August 1914 the colony's government called up all its reservists, so that the German military power on New Britain consisted of two officers of the regular army, seven Land Army officers, fifty-two Germans of other ranks on the reserve list and 240 native soldiers.

A German reservist at Rabaul. [Australian War Memorial A2546]

Apart from the topographic and geographical limitations on the defence of the colonies, the Germans were not in a position to command any sizable support or loyalty from the people they governed. In Tsingtao, they had razed the fishing village which stood where the German Navy wanted to build its new city; the Chinese were moved out of the way. A decree allowed the German administration to expropriate land through purchase, and the Germans told the hapless farmers they could soon find jobs in the warehouses and factories which would be built on the land. The navy decided it would not allow Chinese to reside in the German section so that two separate housing districts were laid out — the decision was described as a 'sanitary measure'. Chinese rage at foreign exploiters was growing and the German seizure of this territory had been described as the principal cause of the Boxer Rebellion back in 1900 and its eventual support by the Chinese Government. It did not help the Germans' cause that Shantung province, of which Tsingtao was part, was the birthplace of Confucius and thus had, in Chinese minds, some of the same importance which Christians attribute to the original sites of their religion in Israel. The Germans were viewed as 'infidels'.

Not that this seemed to trouble the Germans very much. They had created at Tsingtao the sort of establishment that made them feel at home on the China coast. They had built a city where previously a mere village had existed, linked it by railway to the interior of China so that passenger ships used the port to disembark Europeans heading for northern China and Peking. Sewerage and water were laid on. Wide, elegant streets were laid out and imposing homes built along the waterfront. A hospital offered the latest in medical treatment and hygiene.

A correspondent for *The Manchester Guardian* reported in June 1916 recalling Tsingtao during the German occupation. The Germans had built three good hotels, lined the streets and covered surrounding hills with trees, he wrote. While saying the architecture was a little too 'café Gothic' for his taste, the report conceded

> With the exception of the Peak district in Hong Kong, it is the nearest approach to a garden city on the China coast. The streets are wide, the road surfaces excellent. The houses are none of them mean and all of a cheerful colour with pleasant tiles; nearly all have gardens — a rare virtue in most of the foreign settlements of the Far East.

The British who lived in Peking and Tientsin spent their holidays at the newly acquired colony of Weihaiwei, just across the peninsula from Tsingtao. The Germans found that their own territory offered fine beaches and cool sea breezes in the summer; there was plenty of opportunity for sailing and racing while clubs and hotels provided entertainment and fine cuisine. It was not only the Germans who treasured Tsingtao; it was a favoured resort of many European communities before 1914.

The South Pacific territories were not so attractive although the Germans did what they could, especially in Samoa. This was largely due to Dr Wilhelm Solf, the governor who was in office at Apia from the acquisition of the territory in 1900 until the end of 1911 (and a man, who although not a noble, who would go on to head Germany's Colonial Office). He had learnt the ropes in German East Africa, and showed great eagerness to comprehend the Samoan tradition and way of life. Solf had lived in Samoa for a number of years before Germany acquired the territory and he had come to have a knowledge of and sympathy for the Samoan people (qualities not always evident in his New Zealand successors after 1914). He set about public works, and the planting of rubber and cocoa was rapidly expanded. Chinese indentured labourers were introduced to work on the German plantations.

The Germans also got rid of 'the white men on the beach' — the drifters and beachcombers who found in the Pacific islands the sort of idle existence which suited them. Far from encouraging further colonisation, Solf actually opposed settlement by those who could afford only small plantations; he thought they would become a burden on the colony. The export trade built up under Solf was insignificant for Germany itself, but the increasing revenue from exports of copra and other products allowed the administration to pour money into public works and the trade grew, even though New Zealand's Union Steam Ship Company withdrew from the Samoan service after Germany acquired control.

German sailors pose for the photographer at Tsingtao. This colony was run by and for the German navy. It was the navy that made sure that, each time they came to consider naval matters in the Reichstag, the legislators were inundated with glowing reports about the progress being made at Tsingtao. [AKG–Berlin]

The Imperial dockyard at Tsingtao. The gunboat Jaguar *is in the foreground with* Scharnhorst *at right.* [Paul Schmalenback Collection]

New Guinea was the poor relation. By the time they were thrown out in 1914, the Germans had still never even come into contact with the majority of their subjects. However, they did achieve a great deal more in terms of economic development, public works and education than did the Australians in Papua. (By 1914 the Australians had not even built a public school.)

The failure of this German colony is adduced by the fact that shortly before the war there were only slightly more than 1,100 Europeans living on mainland New Guinea and the Bismarck Archipelago combined. It was hot, covered in jungle, peopled by what were seen at the time as savages and malaria was lying in wait for any European. Hundreds of thousands, probably millions, of marks were pumped into plantations which returned practically nothing. Berlin did not care — it had neither the economic importance of German East Africa, the naval appeal of Tsingtao, nor the emotional tug of Samoa.

But Australia did care about New Guinea. It remembered how the Germans had sneaked in during 1884. It also knew that any German colony, malarial or not, was a safe haven for the Imperial German Navy and, as such, ought to be taken seriously. The New Zealanders had similar fears for Western Samoa — along with the desire to make it the jewel in the crown of New Zealand's Pacific empire.

On the morning of 6 August 1914 a cipher telegraph arrived from the Colonial Secretary in London addressed to the Australian Governor-General:

> If your Ministers desire and feel themselves able to seize German wireless stations at Yap in Marshall Islands, Nauru on Pleasant Island, and New Guinea, we should feel that this was a great and urgent Imperial service. You will, however, realise that any territory now occupied must be at the disposal of the Imperial Government for purposes of an ultimate settlement at conclusion of the war. Other Dominions are acting in a similar way on the same understanding, in particular, suggestion is being made to New Zealand in regard to Samoa.

Australia and New Zealand did not need to be asked a second time. The Dominion governments were behind Britain all the way; the recruits could not wait to sink a bayonet into a German. At the turn of the century, German's Foreign Secretary Prince von Bülow had stated contentedly that 'now Germany's possessions in the South Seas are complete and this treaty (with Spain over the Carolines and Marianas) together with the one with China regarding Kiaochow, are milestones along the same road, the road to Weltpolitik'.

The Australians sailed from Sydney on 19 August. The Australian army force left aboard the armed troopship the *Berrima* which, together with the navy escort, arrived off Herbertshohe on 11 September.

The first naval party which was landed at Herbertshohe encountered no resistance in hoisting the Union Jack. However, the party which set out to find the wireless station at Bita Paka found the Germans were waiting, entrenched at a bend in the road where they had a clear field of fire. Native troops were stationed in coconut palms in the jungle as snipers. So, when the Australians came to the bend in the road they were assailed by heavy rifle fire. Two able seamen were cut down, while the medical corps officer Captain Brian Pockley was mortally wounded — he had given his armband with the red cross to a sailor who was carrying one of the wounded sailors an was therefore not identifiable by the enemy as a medic; Captain Pockley thus became the first Australian officer casualty of the war and was buried at Herbertshohe. Reinforcements were rushed from the Australian ships lying off, and the man who led the renewed charge, Lieutenant-Commander Charles Ewell, was shot dead. The Australians thereupon threatened to start a naval bombardment of Herbertshohe if resistance was not abandoned. The Germans capitulated, but when the Australians advanced the German troops began to run into the bush, several being shot as they tried to escape. A number of Germans and New Guineans were buried on the spot in a hastily dug trench.

The Australians pressed on to the wireless station where they found seven German officials and twenty-six New Guineans who, although armed, surrendered without a fight. Although the station was incomplete — the main lattice masts were still lying on the ground, and only a low-powered transmitter was in use — it was clear that once finished it would have been one of the finest in the Southern Hemisphere. The hilltop site at Bita Paka, had the German soldiers been greater in number and better equipped, would have been extremely difficult to capture; it was surrounded on three sides by wide steep gullies, while the fourth side was a grassy slope totally devoid of any cover for advancing troops. The station captured, the Australian soldiers and naval reservists returned to Herbertshohe. A letter written by one of the men recalls the heat of that day:

> I won't forget that march. I had two hundred rounds of ammunition, a two pound tin of jam, tin of bully, biscuits for two days, a camera and films, with a heliograph hanging round my neck to counterbalance the weight at the back. The heat was oppressive. We silently marched back to our base. I was carrying my rifle at the slope, and I thought I would give the left arm a rest; as I took the rifle away I was amazed to find the left arm remained in the same position, so I knocked it down with the rifle and circulation once more continued'.

The German Governor, Dr Eduard Haber (who had been appointed only in April), was not in Rabaul when the Australians arrived; he was aboard the Government yacht, *Komet*, visiting settlements on the New Guinea mainland. Cruising along the northern coast of Neu Pommern, the vessel received wireless messages which indicated British warships were close. *Komet* crept along the coast at night, sailing without lights, laying up in uncharted harbours during the day. The captain of *Komet* realised there was no point going anywhere near the British or Australians, and changed direction to put as much distance between him and them as possible. At one stage she met up with the *Prinz Eitel Friedrich* at Malakal.

Meanwhile, the radio station put into service by the Australian Army had intercepted messages giving details of troops around Rabaul and Herbertshohe. Australian destroyers were despatched to search the coast of New Britain and to find any ships hiding in harbours or bays. The situation was particularly critical as the *Scharnhorst* and the *Gneisenau* were still at large in the Pacific and the steamer *Moresby* was on its way from Sydney with much-needed supplies for the troops at Rabaul. (Had the Australians known that the *Cormoran*, the *Prinz Eitel Friedrich* and the *Emden* were also on the loose they would have no doubt been horrified at the opportunities for disaster.)

The native people reported to the Australians that there was a ship in a secluded harbour some hundreds of kilometres from Rabaul. The Australians thought this was the most likely source of the wireless traffic, and that the culprit was either the *Komet* or the survey ship *Planet* (which had actually reached Yap by this time). While it was active and at large, there would always be the danger that any German ship could direct von Spee's forces by wireless.

The Australians had captured the German governor's small steam yacht the *Nusa* (as well as five other island steamers) and she was commissioned to hunt down the *Komet*, being equipped with a wireless set, a four-pounder gun in the bows and a twelve-pounder aft. A crew of thirty was pulled together consisting of naval gun crews, an army machine gun section and six infantrymen. It left Rabaul early on the morning of 9 October. The *Nusa* weighed only seventy tons, leaving a considerable disparity in size between hunter and quarry. Further interrogation of the natives along the coast directed the Australians toward the *Komet*. However, sentries were left behind to stop the natives taking to their canoes to warn the enemy.

At first light the next morning, and with a thick mist to obscure her approach, the *Nusa* sailed into the secluded harbour to find the *Komet* lying at anchor, the captain and other crew members still in their bunks. The first the German captain knew of the *Nusa's* presence was when an Australian colonel climbed aboard demanding the *Komet's* surrender. The captain was angry that he had been taken without a fight — all he could say was 'I was taken quite unawares. Had I seen the little *Nusa* coming she would have been under water now'. The *Komet* was taken to Rabaul, then to Sydney, renamed *Una* and returned to New Guinea as a gunboat of the Royal Australian Navy.

The German government yacht Komet *which eluded the Australians for some days until surprised by a small force chasing it aboard the* Nusa *(shown in inset).* [Australian War Memorial 301596]

The *Komet* capture was part of the mopping-up to be done after the capture of Rabaul and Herbertshohe. No resistance was offered when the Australians landed on the New Guinea mainland, nor at Kavieng in New Ireland. Nauru was occupied on 6 November (with its then estimated £400 million worth of phosphate deposits). The Germans were arrested and taken off the island. The last territory to be taken was Bougainville which was occupied in early December.

On Samoa, the Germans came quickly to an agreement with the resident British and Chinese nationals that life could go on provided everyone kept the peace. The administrators knew it was only a matter of time before some effort would be made to invade the islands.

Britain wanted as much German territory seized as quickly as possible — there was a chance of the war ending in an early armistice at that stage, and the Imperial Government in London saw its chance to acquire a foothold in its enemy's colonies. That, and the keenness of the New Zealanders to see some action, prompted the rush to Samoa.

New Zealand was champing at the bit. Within four days of London asking the country to occupy Western Samoa, New Zealand had its force of 1,400 organised. On the morning of 12 August, the men marched through a cold and rainy Wellington to board the Union Steam Ship Company vessels *Monowai* and *Moeraki* which had been commandeered as troopships. A holiday in the capital was declared, on 14 August and the troops came ashore for a final parade. Great crowds lined the Wellington streets as the men marched to the Basin Reserve (the city's main cricket ground) where they were given a great official farewell. None of the troops knew where they were going; they had surfboats, which suggested a landing, but they were also equipped with the heaviest underwear and thick woollen uniforms. As the troopships slid out of Wellington Harbour on the morning of 15 August, the sea calm and the sky clear, the two third class cruisers the *Psyche* and the *Philomel* joined the convoy as escorts, with the *Pyramus* falling in later.

First landfall was Noumea in the French colony of New Caledonia. It had been intended that the convoy should sail directly to Fiji where it would meet up with Australian warships given that New Zealand had only its pathetic and ageing cruisers as protection. But Australia was unable to provide an escort onward from Suva at such short notice, and so the convoy was diverted to Noumea where it waited for *Australia* and the French cruiser *Montcalm*. Even so, travelling as far as Noumea with a naval escort that would be useless if confronted by one of the German cruisers was a rather silly risk. Luckily for the New Zealanders, von Spee was in fact thousands of kilometres away to the north with pressing problems of his own, as will be explained in the next chapter. From Noumea, the enlarged fleet eventually moved off with the two troopships astern of the *Australia,* the *Psyche*, the *Philomel* and the *Montcalm* to port and the *Pyramus* and the *Melbourne* guarding the starboard flank. At night the escorts closed to single file with the *Psyche* scouting ahead.

When, on the morning 30 August 1914, the fleet reached its destination, the soldiers were primed for action. The *Psyche* sailed through the reef, swept the harbour at Apia for mines and sent a landing party ashore with a letter demanding the surrender of the Germans. The reply was ambiguous: there would be no surrender, nor would there be any resistance. Crowds of Europeans gathered around the landing party to find out what was happening. It was more like a courtesy naval visit in atmosphere than an enemy invasion.

New Zealand soldiers march through Apia after landing unopposed in German Samoa, August 1914 [Alexander Turnbull Library]

The German flag was hauled down and government offices were taken over by the New Zealanders. Governor Erich Schultz-Ewerth and his officials were placed on the New Zealand cruisers to be taken to Auckland as prisoners of war. Two days later, the navy steamed away leaving the army to its own devices. It was hardly the stuff of military legend, particularly when the troops found that their main duties in Samoa were to dig trenches, build roads and bridges and, when there was no work, to drill or be sent on route marches. There was considerable illness among the New Zealand soldiers. The sun glared down with all its tropical heat on the New Zealanders in their heavy underwear and woollen uniforms.

There was the occasional excitement. On the morning of 14 September two large warships appeared on the horizon. It was

Scharnhorst and *Gneisenau*. Von Spee, on hearing that Apia had fallen, hoped he might find ships anchoring there which could be picked off by the guns of his two heavy cruisers. Alas, there was nothing remaining but a small sailing boat. The troops on the shore were at action stations expecting a bombardment to begin at any moment. No shots were fired, but the two German ships steamed back and forth near Apia for nearly four hours while the land forces waited tensely. What the New Zealanders did not know was that the von Spee was loathe to waste his ammunition, and eventually he steamed off to the south in order to mislead his enemy as to his real destination; once over the horizon, the two ships turned slowly toward Tahiti.

A week later eleven German sailors rowed into Apia harbour still believing that it was in German hands. They were part of the crew of the unfortunate *Elsass*, the freighter which had fled Sydney on the eve of war six weeks earlier only to be interned in Pago Pago by the Americans; there they seized a cutter and set out for Apia thinking it was still German territory. They were promptly arrested and sent to New Zealand.

With the Germans expelled from the South Pacific — at least in terms of land occupation — Australia and New Zealand turned their attention toward helping Britain. The British were not as keen to provide help in return, suggesting to New Zealand Prime Minister William Massey that his country's contingent should be sent across the Tasman to join the Australians with only the *Philomel* as escort. It was, the Admiralty said, perfectly safe. With great and grave reluctance the New Zealanders agreed to comply, and two troopships sailed from Auckland on 24 September. Later in the day the Governor-General of Australia sent an urgent cable to Massey warning him that the transports were possibly in serious danger. Massey immediately had the ships recalled. The New

Zealand authorities decided to wait until the middle of October by which time the British armoured cruiser, the *Minotaur,* and the Japanese cruiser, the *Ibuki,* arrived to provide a more reliable escort.

By this time the *Scharnhorst* and the *Gneisenau* had sailed toward South America after bombarding Papeete. Only the *Emden* remained as a threat.

4

Emden!

SMS Emden. [Paul Schmalenbach Collection]

THE BAND HAD PLAYED *Watch on the Rhine* as the sun rose over Tsingtao on the morning of 31 July as war was spreading in Europe and the light cruiser *Emden* cast off its mooring lines. The sailors left behind cheered from the wharves, other men waved their hats and women cried as the *Emden* had pulled out of Tsingtao for what would be the last time. Her officers and crew had little time to reflect on the probability that they would never again see the shores of Tsingtao, nor eat cakes with coffee at the Cafe Metropol. That first evening at sea a Japanese mail steamer spotted the German ship and immediately radioed the presence of the cruiser as 'on course 135 degrees, approximately 190 miles from Tsingtao'. The German ship's course was immediately altered and speed improved. As he would for most of his last cruise aboard the *Emden*, Captain Karl von Müller spent most of his time on the bridge. Comfortable chairs had been placed there, where he could sleep between action or emergencies. He spent most of his waking hours studying charts. Below the bridge, lookouts were added during the hours of darkness, while gun and torpedo crews were always kept ready for action.

The *Emden's* extraordinary success — although short-lived — would be due largely to this man. According to the accounts of officers aboard the ship, von Müller was regarded almost with reverence by his crew. Karl von Müller was retiring by nature, being shy and withdrawn since childhood. The son of a militia officer, he had risen from naval cadet and seen service on many ships, including the pre-dreadnought battleship *Kaiser Wilhelm II* where he served as gunnery officer in 1903. However, his progress through the ranks was slow and it was not until 1912, when he was nearly forty years old, that he was given the *Emden*, his first, and last, command.

The ship herself was a light cruiser designed, not to fight other warships, but to disrupt merchant shipping. She had ten 105-millimetre guns, which were sufficient to subdue anything other than an opposing cruiser; she could make nearly twenty-five knots, which allowed her to catch and overhaul any merchantman then afloat, and she could travel for 9,000 kilometres without re-coaling if she kept to a low speed. Among von Müller's officers was the extrovert Lauterbach, the debonair Prinz Franz Joseph of Hohenzollern who was a nephew of the Kaiser and now second torpedo officer and, as chief officer, Kapitanleutnant Hellmuth von Mücke. Von Mücke was a professional naval man, tall and slender with brown hair and blue eyes, who embodied all the attributes of the German military man. He was the most Anglophobic of the officers and persistently raged against the British. He had been commander of a destroyer in home waters before being assigned to the East Asiatic Squadron. While a strict disciplinarian, he was also a man of considerable intelligence and ability. After the *Emden's* end, he was to show both those attributes.

By 12 August *Emden* reached her rendezvous point in the Caroline Islands. In an interview in 1917, von Mücke described his ship arriving at the Caroline and taking 'up a berth near the flagship amidst the cheers of the squadron. All three ships (the *Scharnhorst* and *Gneisenau* presumably being the others) were busy coaling from colliers, and in their neighbourhood lay a large number of auxiliary vessels". The following morning saw the squadron head for sea, in line ahead; at midday, von Spee signalled Emden to proceed independently. The previous day had seen von Müller suggest to his admiral that the ship be sent to the Indian Ocean.

After farewelling von Spee and his squadron, von Müller set course for Malayan waters, accompanied by the collier *Markomannia*. *Emden* tried to raise the German wireless station on Yap, but by this time the *Hampshire,* the *Yarmouth* and the *Minotaur* had shelled it out of action. So the two German ships headed for Angaur Island in the Palau group and the German phosphate operation where another collier was due to meet them and provide more fuel.

Instead, on 20 August, they met the Norddeutscher-Lloyd mail steamer *Prinzess Alice* carrying a number of soldiers, sailors and reservists. The passenger vessel had been heading for Manila and had been diverted on von Müller's orders. Several of the sailors were transferred to the *Emden* along with supplies. *Prinzess Alice* was then ordered to follow the *Emden* to sea, but there was a fault with her boilers and von Müller despatched her to the Philippine port of Cebu. Next day, it was the turn of the antiquated light cruiser *Geier* to rendezvous with the *Emden*. This painfully slow and poorly armed gunboat had been advised of the war's start only two days earlier due to problems with its radio equipment.

Von Müller ordered her back to Angaur to try and locate two colliers which could then sail to meet the *Emden,* and she was then ordered to go on to Yap to try and defend it if the wireless station had been repaired. After that, *Geier* should try and catch up with von Spee's squadron. After a number of calls to find the colliers and after hearing that the *Planet* was already at Yap, the *Geier's* commander set his wallowing gunboat on course for Majuro Island in the Marshalls. The combination of poor coal, faulty boilers and a fouled bottom restricted her to seven knots. She was to reach the island two weeks after the squadron had left this part of the Pacific. The ship was then due to head for the United States for internment but, even though her collier took her in tow in order to save fuel, poor *Geier* was able to go only as far as Honolulu, and was interned there.

Meanwhile, the *Emden* had crossed the equator on 22 August passing through the Molucca Passage and was heading for Dutch Timor where she was due to meet a collier three days later. The collier did not keep the meeting, the Dutch observing neutrality and ordering it away before *Emden* arrived, so von Müller was forced to take nearly 500 tons of coal from the *Markomannia*, the refuelling having to take place off the coast of the Portuguese end of the island. The Dutch were particularly anxious to keep out of the war; they did not want to suffer Belgium's fate at the hands of the Germans. The captain of the Dutch warship *Marten Harpertzoon Tromp* received von Müller aboard where he imparted the news that the Dutch had ordered the collier away. 'I am sorry. You cannot coal here', he stated simply. After von Müller had returned to his ship, the *Tromp* escorted the Germans out of territorial waters. The *Emden* headed east, then cut back on to a westerly course once she was out of sight of the Dutch.

Meanwhile, von Mücke had had an idea — disguise. Every British ship would be on the lookout for the *Emden* and its three tell-tale funnels. British cruisers had four: three round and one oval. Overnight the *Emden* was transformed by the addition of a fourth 'funnel' made of canvas initially, then replaced with sail cloth on a lattice frame; now, at least at a distance, she could be mistaken for the *Yarmouth* which was also in the area. The new addition was painted grey and when necessary could spew chemically-produced smoke.

The air was thick with the wireless traffic from British ships. The *Hampshire,* although von Müller did know of it at the time, was perilously close. The Germans meanwhile steamed up the coast of Java and Sumatra, keeping out of sight of the coast, crossing the equator again on 3 September and then moved into the Bay of Bengal.

The coal in the bunkers was getting low again. Von Müller had to find somewhere he could safely come alongside the *Markomannia* to transfer more coal. That place was Simalur, a small island in the lee of Sumatra now called Pulau Simeulucut, which she reached on 4 September. The *Hampshire* had been at the same spot the previous day. The bay was perfect for the Germans because it offered anchorages which could not been seen from the open sea. As usual, the coaling was backbreaking work, all 1,000 tons of it. The transfer began in the morning, but the men had to stop work as the day got hotter and hotter. They restarted later in the day and carried on until just before midnight, the job still unfinished. The men slept on deck that night; after the punishing heat of the coal holds, they could not face sleeping in airless cabins. The work began again at first light.

Once more, the Dutch found them out. The Dutch official aboard a government vessel which had turned into the bay pointed out that they had already overstayed the twenty-four limit in Dutch waters. The Germans managed to stall by saying they needed two hours to raise steam. The Dutch benignly agreed to that extension, taking advantage of the hospitality in the wardroom until the deadline arrived. Von Müller was anxious to avoid being bottled up in harbour, and so the two German ships steamed out to sea before the deadline expired. The exhausted crews, who had been looking forward to a rest once the coaling was done, had to turn to immediately and prepare their ships for sea. But now the *Emden* was at last in the Indian Ocean and ready for action.

*   *   *

The *Emden's* fighting career lasted a bare two months. On 10 September 1914 she captured her first prize; by 9 November the cruiser was a wreck on the shoals of Cocos Island.

Just before midnight on 9 September, the *Emden* spotted the 4,000 ton Greek steamer *Pontoporos*, carrying Bengal coal from Calcutta to Bombay. The Germans could not make out who she was in the dark, but put two shots across the ship's bow, at the same time sending in Morse on the lamp: 'Stop your engines. Don't use wireless.' This instruction was obeyed aboard the other vessel. Lauterbach was boarding officer and described the scene on the Greek ship's bridge. 'My God', the Greek captain said, 'a German cruiser here'. The captain protested that the ship was a Greek neutral but Lauterbach was delighted to see that the coal was consigned to the Indian government and therefore could be seized as contraband by a belligerent. 'Thank you very much', said Lauterbach, 'you are captured'. For the Germans, to have let the Greek ship go would been fatal: as soon as it reached an Indian port, the British would be on *Emden's* trail.

The Germans also found a recent edition of an English-language Calcutta newspaper (presumably *The Statesman*) which was still reporting shipping movements. For von Müller and his crew it was just a matter of picking which ships they wanted to intercept, and waiting astride the main shipping lane until their intended victims sailed over the horizon. While the cargo aboard *Pontoporos* could legally be seized, the ship itself was still neutral and therefore could not be taken as a prize. The middle of the Bay of Bengal was no place to be transhipping coal. The matter was resolved when the Greek captain was persuaded that German money was just as good as British, and that he should now consider himself under charter to the German government. That settled, the ungainly fleet made its way toward the steamer lanes.

There were plenty of potential victims from which to choose. India's vast resources had been quickly marshalled to the aid of the empire, and a massive number of ships — tankers, troopships, everything from the sleek and speedy mail steamers to the ageing tramps — were pressed into service to collect men, horses and equipment from Calcutta, Bombay, Karachi, Madras and other Indian ports and then deliver them to the European, Middle East and East African theatres of war.

One of these vessels was the *Indus*, a 4,000 ton passenger-cargo ship en route from Calcutta to France via Bombay under Indian government charter and which had been converted at the former port into a troop transport. She was fully bunkered, well provisioned for the troops who would join her in Bombay, and was carrying extra lifeboats. The *Indus* sailed peacefully down the Bay of Bengal for three days but then smoke appeared over the southern horizon. Not even a ripple of alarm was felt on the bridge; her skipper, Captain Henry Smaridge, could be forgiven the assumption he had sighted a British cruiser attached to the East Indies station in Ceylon. The *Indus* crew were bathing on deck, and they all stopped to look at the fast ship, smoke pouring from her four funnels, as she bore quickly down upon them. Meanwhile, on the *Emden's* bridge, there were jokes about how they needed to find a prize carrying plenty of soap. Most of the ship's supplies had been exhausted after the coaling at Simalur.

The ships closed, still without alarm on the part of the British vessel. Although the *Emden* was flying no flag, she also had the fake funnel which had given her the appearance of a Royal Navy cruiser. As the *Emden* came broadside on to the *Indus* there was a sudden flash from one of the cruiser's guns and a few seconds later a shell whined over the *Indus* bridge and fell into the sea beyond. Simultaneously, the German ensign streaked to the top of the *Emden's* stern flagpole while signal flags warning the *Indus* not to use her wireless cracked in the breeze. The transport ship hove to and waited to be boarded although the opportunity to burn confidential papers was taken before the Germans arrived. The *Indus*, while sailing in ballast, was under orders to carry troops and horses (in special horse boxes on deck) from Bombay to France, so she was clearly an enemy military vessel. Von Müller had none of the qualms he had experienced in deciding what to do with his Greek catch. Most importantly for the crew, there was news that among other supplies the *Indus* had a huge supply of soap aboard. Clearly, von Müller could not sit in the middle of one of Britain's busiest imperial shipping lanes and calmly transfer coal. Taking the *Indus* along was also out of the question. It was therefore decided that she would have to be sunk; but not before all moveable items had been transferred. Several members of the *Indus* crew were pressed into service to help load liquor, cigarettes, anything that could be packed (including the soap), a chronometer and navigation instruments aboard the German ship.

By midday the *Markomannia* had arrived on the scene, and she in turn was followed by the 'grimy little tramp of the common type' as one British seafarer described the *Pontoporos,* under Lauterbach's command. The crew of the *Indus* were thereupon transferred to the *Markomannia,* where they were offered a meal and whisky, while the booty was being transferred to the cruiser. By mid-afternoon, von Müller decided it was time to go. A sinking party, consisting of an engineer, and four stokers, went aboard the Indus and opened the sea-cocks. By the time this party had returned to *Emden* the British transport steamer was still obstinately afloat. Von Müller ordered several shells to be pumped into her to help her on her way; still she would not sink. At last, after an hour, the water finally rose over her bulwarks and she slowly rolled over to starboard. The additional lifeboats broke loose as the ship went down, and floated over the spot like marker buoys. There was no time to sink them even though they were incriminating evidence of what had happened as they bobbed about in the gathering dusk.

The *Emden* did not have to wait long for her next victim — the 6,000 ton *Lovat,* also on her way to Bombay to pick up troops for France. The captain, Lauterbach said, was another old friend of his from the China seas, a man of about sixty years of age and who would probably never get another command. There was no time to comb the ship for supplies; her crew were taken quickly across to the *Markomannia* (which had again been temporarily left behind as the *Emden* worked up to full speed to pursue new quarry) and the sea-cocks opened. The *Lovat* proved to be as stubborn as the *Indus,* and even a shelling failed to hasten her progress. Night had fallen by the time *Lovat* finally went down.

Between actions, life aboard the *Emden* was pretty much the same as in peacetime, except that the ship was constantly primed for action. Although the woodwork in the officers' mess had been removed and curtains taken down, the officers lived the style of life they were used to, especially with the liquor, chocolates and cigarettes taken off the *Indus.* In Hellmuth von Mücke's account of the *Emden's* exploits he recalls that the most pleasant hours were always those spent reading the newspapers which had been captured from enemy steamers, even though they inevitably reported the war from the British point of view. 'For instance', he wrote, 'we found it very reassuring to discover, by consulting the map, that the *"retreat* of the Germans from France" which the (Reuter News) Agency had declared to amount "almost to a rout" had proceeded in a *westerly* direction'.

The crew was constantly busy keeping the engines and guns in top condition. Shower baths made out of old pipe had been rigged up on deck, and each man could shower three times a day, a great relief in the tropical heat. Each afternoon the ship's band gave a concert, some of the men singing, others dancing to the music, others just smoking cigarettes and listening. At night, the men would sing well known songs, the refrains wafting out into the dark ocean sky, the favourite being *Watch on the Rhine.* Monotonous diets were a common feature on warships of the period when on long voyages. Not so with Emden: she had kept to herself the best supplies from ships she captured. Von Mücke describes hams and sausages dangling from an engine room skylight, stacks of chocolate and confectionery, bottles of claret and three-star brandy. Chocolate and bonbons were served with afternoon coffee, and the booty had also included a quarter of a million cigarettes. Plentiful supplies of flour were turned daily into fresh bread. The boarding crews soon became skilled at picking the items that would be needed by their comrades, from soldering lamps to machine oil. However, von Mücke said he drew the line at collecting oil paintings, large mirrors and other indulgences. 'So we spent the passing days, while certain death lurked round about us', he remembered. The crew of the *Emden* had few illusions about their ultimate fate.

Like a moth to a light, von Müller was drawn nearer to the rich pickings of Calcutta and the Hooghly River, down which the Bengal pilots guided ships to the open sea, many of them into von Müller's lap. On 12 September, the *Emden* found her next prize late that evening. The Germans still had a few days' grace before the alarm over the *Indus* and *Lovat* would be raised.

Out of the darkness came the *Kabinga,* a 4,750 ton British merchant steamer sailing from Calcutta. The *Emden's* signal lamp blinked out the orders to stop and not to use the wireless. The prize crew went aboard and sent back to the cruiser by lamp the news that they had boarded a British ship belonging to the Ellermen and Bucknall Steamship Company of London, that she was bound for New York via Port Said with a cargo for an American company. This posed a problem. The ship could under the rules of war be seized, but the cargo, being neutral, could not. If von Müller sent the vessel to the bottom, Germany would have to compensate the American owners of the cargo. The matter was resolved when the German commander discovered the English master had his wife and child aboard. The decision was taken to keep the *Kabinga* as a dump for all the prisoners, and those from the *Lovat* and *Indus* were transferred to her. The ship was placed under one of the prize officers, Oberleutnant von Levetzow.

The motley flotilla was soon briefly joined by yet another ship. She was the *Killin,* a 3,625 ton collier, carrying 6,000 tons of Indian coal from Calcutta to Colombo. By the time his prisoners had come up on deck, that morning of 13 September, von Müller had already decided the *Killin's* fate. The variety of Indian coal first found on the *Pontoporos* and now on the *Killin* was too soft for the *Emden* — it clogged up her boilers and slowed the cruiser down too much. There was little delay in coming to the decision to sink the collier. At mid-morning, the *Emden* signalled the other ships to stop, the prize crew was taken aboard the cruiser and replaced by the sinking party. This time, their work went well and, with a few well-placed shells she went under quickly. Von Müller now turned north-east.

Next came the *Diplomat,* a 7,767 ton Harrison liner carrying 10,000 tons of tea from Calcutta to Liverpool. There was nothing von Müller wanted from her and bombs were placed aboard, blowing her apart. The liner's skipper, Captain Robert Thomson, later told of what members of the German crew had let slip in conversation; that von Müller had kept his tactics and plans to himself, and that not even his own officers had the slightest idea where they would be going from one moment to another. They received their orders, carried them out, and their commander alone knew their final objective.

The day of 13 September was proving to be busy. With the *Killin* and *Diplomat* already consigned to the floor of the ocean since dawn, the *Emden's* tired crew were called out again when a steamer belching huge quantities of smoke came into view. She was the Italian *Loredano,* bound from Genoa to Calcutta. Italy was neutral at this stage of the war and the ship was not carrying any contraband cargo. The Italian master refused von Müller's request, relayed by way of the officers in the boarding party, to take all the

British prisoners still aboard the *Kabinga*. Eventually the skipper was talked around, but by this time it was getting dark and there was a rising swell. The *Loredano* was allowed to proceed on her way. There seems little question that the Italian captain had scant love for Germany; he was discourteous to the officers who came aboard and although he promised not to raise the alarm there was little doubt in the *Emden's* wardroom that he would tell the first ship he saw of the German's presence — which is exactly what happened.

The Germans knew therefore that there was little point keeping the prisoners any longer. Late in the afternoon of 14 September they captured a collier in ballast sailing for Calcutta, the 4,110 ton *Trabboch*. She was quickly sunk and her crew joined their fellows on the prison ship. The prisoners had already been brought together and told they would be freed and put aboard the *Kabinga* under her original commander, Captain Smaridge. As the *Kabinga* swung away from the *Emden* and the other two ships, the now released captives lined the decks and cheered the departing Germans in gratitude for the meticulous and fair treatment they had received at the hands of von Müller's crew.

The surface fleets of the German navy normally behaved honourably with regard to international law during World War I and, while atrocities were common on land, there were few committed by the surface fleets. (In 1939, at the height of Nazi contempt for international law, British captives aboard the pocket battleship *Graf Spee* were to report how well they had been treated within the limitations of captivity below decks in a warship.)

The *Emden's* last prize in these waters was the *Clan Mathieson*: heading for Calcutta with a cargo of steam locomotives, Rolls-Royce motorcars and two horses. The horses were destroyed and the ship was sunk. Emden then turned for Rangoon after coaling from the *Pontoporos*. She despatched the slow Greek collier back to Simalur Island. The ship was too slow and was holding back the German cruiser now that the *Hampshire* and other Royal Navy ships were on its tail. The crew of the *Clan Mathieson* were placed aboard the Norwegian freighter, the *Dovre,* which was intercepted two days later, and despatched to the Burmese capital.

Von Müller knew the British were after him simply by tuning the *Emden's* wireless to the frequencies used by Indian shore stations and British ships. These messages also gave him a fair idea where the enemy vessels actually were. For a time, the *Emden* had been able to go about her business with reasonable safety. Few merchantmen had wireless sets in 1914 and therefore they could not send out distress signals when captured. At the most, port authorities at their destinations would give these vessels an extra forty-eight hours to allow for bad weather or a mechanical fault at sea, before raising the alarm.

By contrast, most warships were equipped with radio so that once the presence of a raider had been established, every naval unit in the Bay of Bengal would soon know about it. Now the *Emden* would have to out-think the enemy moment by moment, con-stantly changing course to try and throw the pursuers off her track. So it was, on 14 September, that the wireless operator at Calcutta nearly jumped off his chair when he received the message from the *Loredano,* relayed by a British warship, that a German cruiser was in the Bay of Bengal. Von Müller knew that the Norwegian captain of the *Dovre* would report him as soon as he sailed into Rangoon. This would draw the British forces to the area. The net had to be slipped.

The *Emden* made a sharp turn, coaled from the *Markomannia* and headed straight back across the Bay of Bengal toward Madras where vast oil tanks lined the foreshore. The Germans reasoned that shipping in the bay would evaporate while the raider was about and that they could sail for days on the sea lanes without finding a prize. Von Müller also knew the French and Japanese had now joined the search for his ship and that any of these major British, French or Japanese warships had the capacity to blow the *Emden* out of the water.

In the early evening of 22 September, at full action stations, the *Emden,* closed on Madras. As Prince Franz Joseph wrote:

> Towards eight o'clock the Madras light came in sight. We were astounded that this was still burning, proving the unwatchfulness of the English authorities. They cannot have expected, and must have taken it to be impossible, that a fortified harbour should be attacked by 'impudent Germans' ... On approaching the town we had another surprise. The harbour lights were all burning, and the whole town was a sea of light. How different it was in Germany and on German coasts, where at the beginning of war all lights and lighthouses were extinguished, and no coastal town showed a light towards the sea.

The *Emden* steamed in at high speed and fixed her searchlights on the oil tanks. The guns boomed flame and salvoes went screeching toward the tanks. At least one tank exploded immediately, others burst into flame. Fortunately for the inhabitants of the city, the flames were blown seaward by the wind rather than on to the town itself. For a fortified harbour, Madras put up little fight. The Germans had feared the raking gunfire of Fort St George with its 150-millimetre guns, but the only hostile fire fell about 100 metres short of the *Emden,* and probably came from a gun emplacement on the harbour mole. As the tanks of the Burmah

Oil Company blazed high into the night sky, the *Emden* turned toward the harbour entrance. Carefully still showing her port lights she headed north, then, darkening ship, she turned toward the south. Behind her, for all the destruction she had wrought, mercifully only five people had been killed.

The Germans had hoped to give the French at Pondicherry, the main French enclave on the Indian coast, a whipping while they were about it. Early the next morning, the *Emden* steamed slowly past the French colony (one of five along India's coast) looking, unsuccessfully, for ships which could be surprised. The ports of British India and Ceylon, meanwhile, were full of ships which were not prepared to take the risk of meeting the German raider at sea. The only vessels which were venturing out were warships, and they were combing the seas day and night for the *Emden*. The search intensified, diversions of merchant shipping increased and vital troop convoys to feed the Allied war machine were delayed. The pack of hounds after the *Emden* included seven British ships as well as three Japanese vessels and the Russian cruiser *Askold*, immediately recognisable by its five funnels.

Von Müller staggered them all by sinking still more ships. The world was now reading daily newspaper reports of his exploits. Apart from the nightmare of running into a British or allied warship, von Müller and his officers had yet another problem: they were fast running out of coal. Practically none was left in the *Markomannia's* holds, and the coal they had taken from the *Pontoporos* would be of no use if they had to work up to top speed. The chief engineer prayed for a meeting with a British ship carrying the best Welsh coal, the most prized coal in the shipping world. It was not just speed and range that were affected by the use of poor coal, it also meant much harder work for the stokers who had one of the least enviable tasks at the best of times.

The *Emden's* best hope was for her to come across one of the colliers which ferried coal to British naval bases, particularly Singapore and Hong Kong. Von Müller was tempted to turn and head for his assignation at Simalur with the *Pontoporos,* but instead he inched around the southern coast of Ceylon. Keeping about twenty nautical miles from land and, using the little Shantung coal from Tsingtao that was left (because it produced the least smoke) he drifted into the busy Colombo-Penang-Singapore shipping lane. It was example of von Müller's luck that he had not yet been seen by the Japanese light cruiser *Chikuma* which was patrolling the northern Ceylonese coast.

In the middle of the day of 25 September, a smudge of smoke was sighted dead ahead. A few hours later, the British vessel *King Lud* (3,723 tons) which had been travelling in ballast from Alexandria to Calcutta was sinking; its fresh food having been taken off (along with its crew) to replenish supplies aboard the *Emden.* Later that night, Franz Joseph noted that Colombo's sky was lit up by searchlights scanning the horizon. Shortly after, another British ship appeared out of the dark. The Hohenzollern prince was fascinated by the placement of the funnel aft, a relatively unknown design of a ship at that time. By midnight, the British steamer *Tymeric* (3,380 tons) was on her way to the bottom still carrying her cargo of sugar which had been loaded at Semarang in the Dutch East Indies and bound for Falmouth. The crew barely had the chance to catch some sleep before another prize offered itself. This was the 4,525 ton *Gryfevale,* in ballast, and she had been within a tantalisingly short distance of her destination at Colombo when she was caught. She was added to von Müller's little fleet, and the crews of the two sunken vessels were put aboard her.

Captain David Harris of the *King Lud,* upon being later released, expressed no resentment toward the Germans, except for the loss of his ship. He said the captives were well treated on the *Markomannia*. He had been given a cabin to himself, and his officers accommodated two to a room. While the crew of twenty-seven Europeans and two Arabs were taken away from their vessel in the cutter, the armed boarding party, now highly efficient at sending steamers to the bottom, placed mines in numbers two and four holds and then opened the sea-cocks. Captain John Tulloch of the *Tymeric* said he had been given ten minutes to leave his ship, so he had ordered the crew to swing the boats out and gather what clothes they could. Most of the crew of Europeans and lascars were taken to the *Markomannia,* but Tulloch and his chief engineer were sent aboard the cruiser itself where they were given deck chairs on the quarter-deck. It seemed to him that the Germans were now totally dependent on food captured from other ships. Tulloch was given whisky and soda, a pack of cards and books, and was allowed to listen to the ship's band. At breakfast, he was highly amused when the German steward asked him in very good English what he would have for breakfast; they had only pan-cakes and ham left. He felt that the German crew members were 'pretty well fed up'.

Captain William Gibson of the *Foyle,* a 4,147-ton British steamer en route to Rangoon in ballast, was given twenty minutes to leave his ship and demanded longer, but he showed the boarding party where the ship's stores were kept. Nevertheless, he reported the Germans as being 'exceptionally courteous' and he joined in three cheers for the Germans when all the captured crews on the *Gryfevale* were later directed to steam for Colombo and freedom. The same day the 3,570 ton *Ribera* was steaming from Glasgow via Alexandria bound for Batavia (Djakarta) in ballast and was turning toward Colombo to bunker when she was found by the *Emden.* 'My God,' Captain John Isdale later recalled saying, 'the next instant

I saw the German flag being run up and I said "We are finished"!'
He reported that the *Emden* was very dirty. Apparently the sailors'
'whites' were rather less so by this time. The Germans did have
some laundry soap left because they issued bars of Sunlight to the
British officers. They were amused to read in one of the English
papers found aboard the *Tymeric* an advertisement stating that one
particular brand of soap must be good because the crew of the
Emden had taken it from the *Indus* and used it.

But the greatest catch for the raider was in the early hours of
27 September. The little British collier *Buresk*, carrying more than
6,500 tons of first class Cardiff coal, destined for Admiral Jerram's
ships at Hong Kong, sailed into von Müller's clutches. For the
moment, the *Emden's* luck was holding, and she now had a new
supply collier. Von Müller realised he had to get away from this
region of rich pickings — the late arrival of any ship would now
raise the alarm, and the warships could not be far away. By the
Tuesday, 29 September, the *Emden, Markomannia* and *Buresk* sidled
into the Maldive Islands. While the cruiser and her old faithful
retainer made fast alongside each other, the dregs of coal were
scraped from the bottom of the *Markomannia's* holds and carried
aboard the *Emden*. The heat, as usual, was appalling and the hard
work went on until 11 pm. Next day the *Buresk* took oil and fresh
water from the now near-empty German collier. The cruiser's
crew, meanwhile, sat and wrote letters home which would be
posted when the *Markomannia* reached the Dutch East Indies. Her
orders were to seek out the *Pontoporos*, take the coal from her, set
the Greek ship free and then to buy food at Padang in Sumatra.
She was then to meet up at Cocos Island along with any other
colliers she could locate. There was an emotional farewell as the
Markomannia pulled away, and the *Emden* turned south for the
Chagos Archipelago (then part of the colony of Mauritius and

now the British Indian Ocean Territory) both to give the crew a rest in less perilous waters, and also to explore the possibility of catching empty troopships bound for Australia or to intercept ships coming from Australia with refrigerated meat. The ship also badly needed some maintenance, particularly the engines which needed overhauling.

On the island of Diego Garcia a minor but, in retrospect, bizarre incident took place. The island was, of course, British territory and when the cruiser and her captured British collier dropped anchor in the harbour a boat put out from shore. In it was the deputy-manager of the local coconut plantation who, because the mail and papers came only twice a year aboard a schooner from Mauritius, had not heard about the war. Handed a large whisky and soda, he explained that he was always glad to see Germans 'especially those that came in their fine warships'. He had not seen one since 1889 when the frigates *Bismarck* and *Marie* had called. He hoped it would not be as long again before another German ship anchored at Diego Garcia. The Germans saw no point in disabusing him of this feeling of goodwill, especially since they might need to use this harbour again. The guest was a little taken aback by the condition of the *Emden with* the deck covered in oil stains and coal dust, and the railing bent and broken. He observed that the guns had thick matting to protect their crews from flying splinters and that the officers' mess, where he was enjoying his drink, was remarkably bare of furnishings. Von Mücke explained that the cruiser was on a voyage around the world and that it had been necessary to dispense with everything not strictly necessary and that all available space was needed for coal, an explanation which became more plausible with several generous pourings of liquor. The only real problem was that the resident was craving news of the outside world, and they could hardly show the man the

English language newspapers that were on board. So the officers did what they could to invent items of news, as well as mention those points which had no connection with the war. Their visitor was particularly pleased to hear that Pope Pius X had died.

For the crew there was not much time for leisure in this quiet tropical backwater. Coal had to be loaded from the *Buresk,* while other men were set to scrape the *Emden's* bottom. This was achieved by letting enough water into one side of the cruiser to induce a list, thus exposing part of the hull normally under water. The sailors then set to work scraping off the thick layer of mussels and repainting her. The process was then repeated on the other side. This careening gave the *Emden* a little extra speed in an emergency. After work the main relaxation was fishing, lines being dangled from the two ships when time allowed. To the amazement of the Germans, a weird variety of fish was swung on to the cruiser's deck. The ship's doctor insisted on inspecting them before they were cooked as he was aware that some species were not fit to be eaten.

The *Emden* had arrived at Diego Garcia on 9 October. She had just one month to go.

The *Markomannia* had but a few days. As the *Pontoporos* had creaked her way toward Sumatra in late September she had been sighted by the Dutch. The German prize crew had immediately hauled up the Greek flag when they realised they were being studied through glasses.

The next day two Dutch cruisers kept in visual contact, watching carefully. On 6 October the *Markomannia* joined the *Pontoporos* and the coaling began, although the Greek crewmen often had to be made to work at gunpoint. Work was nearing its end on 12 October when the toiling Germans looked up to see a warship heading for them at full speed. They went back to work thinking it was one of the Dutch ships returning. It was the *Yarmouth*. After ordering the *Markomannia's* crew to take to the boats, the British light cruiser thereupon sank her quickly with gun fire. A boarding party took control of the Greek collier.

Meanwhile the German raider was back in business. On 16 October there was another 'three-ship' day. The first victim to be caught, off the northern Maldives island of Minicoy, was the *Clan Grant* in passage to Calcutta with general cargo (including porcelain and typewriters). The boarding party took a copious supply of beer, food, soap and other provisions from her. Lauterbach enjoyed several whiskies and soda with the English captain before the steamer was sunk. Before the work could be completed, another vessel crept into sight. Of all things it was a dredger, the 482 ton *Ponrabbel,* bound for Tasmania from the Clyde to start work for the Marine Board of Launceston. The Germans could not at first make her out, but started to laugh when they realised what she was. The dredge was making about six knots and rolling heavily, Lauterbach describing how the derricks made 'tremendous arcs against the background of the sky'. Getting aboard was not easy with a high sea running. For once Lauterbach was not exaggerating when he said the captain of the dredge welcomed the raider with open arms and told the Germans they could have what they wanted just as long as they took his crew off the rolling platform. He added: 'It's not much fun trying to ride this rolling coffin around the world; and besides, we were paid for the trip before we started from England'. The men had made a previous trip aboard a dredger which had capsized in the Indian Ocean. This second dredger voyage had been due to last four months. The English crew transferred with great delight to the relative comfort of the *Buresk* while the cruiser despatched their nightmare home with a few shells.

The day's work came to an end with the capture and sinking of the British freighter, the two-year-old *Ben Mohr* of 4,806 tons, sailing to Yokohama with general cargo including bicycles and motor vehicles.

Von Müller sighted the Spanish steamer *Fernando Po* but let her pass; it was obvious by the blaze of lights on board, plus the confirmation of identity by signal lamp, that she was a neutral and there was no point *Emden* revealing who she was. British naval intelligence, meanwhile, was advising merchantmen that a course about forty-eight kilometres north of Minicoy Island was 'dead safe'. The captain of the 7,562 ton Blue Funnel vessel *Troilus*, sailing from Colombo to New York with sugar, was therefore furious at having taken this advice, only to fall into the hands of the German raider. Not only was the ship on her maiden voyage but she was carrying an extremely valuable strategic cargo as well as several passengers — one of whom was an old friend of Lauterbach's from the British concession at Shanghai.

That evening, 18 October, the *Emden* captured the cargo steamer *St Egbert* (5,526 tons) and then at midnight the collier *Exford* (4,542 tons) with more than five and half thousand tons of Welsh coal aboard bound for India (the British, having sunk the *Markomannia* and taken the *Pontoporos* were not aware until the middle of October that von Müller had found himself other supplies of coal). The next morning the *Chilkana*, a 5,146-ton passenger-cargo ship bound for Calcutta on her maiden voyage, was nabbed. That day she was sunk, along with the *Troilus*, while the *St Egbert* was despatched to Cochin with her burgeoning complement of prisoners. The *Exford,* with her valuable coal, joined the Germans and was soon detached to wait at Cocos Island. The *Buresk* was afterwards despatched to Simalur.

Von Müller had other fish to fry. Unaware that on 20 October he had passed amazingly close to the cruiser *Hampshire* and her auxiliary, the *Empress of Asia,* the German captain was planning to head for Penang in Malaya. He had learned that it was being used by allied warships and believed he might find the French ships *Montcalm* and *Dupleix* there. They, as it turned out, were elsewhere but ships there were in Penang. The old Russian light cruiser the *Zemtchug* (built 1903, with 120-millimetre guns), was tied up having its boilers scraped; also there were the French destroyers *Pistolet* and *Fronde* (while the third, the *Mousquet* was on patrol at sea), and the French torpedo gunboat, the *D'Iberville.*

On the morning of 28 October, William Brown, Penang pilot, was lying on his long chair aboard his pilot launch in the south channel to Penang harbour when he heard thunder — or, at least, what sounded like thunder-coming out of a clear and crisp morning sky. Then he saw the red flames over the harbour anchorage. 'The *Emden!*' he exclaimed, 'The *Emden* has come!' The Penang authorities had had the jitters about the possibility of a visit from the raider since they had heard about the sinking of the *Indus.*

Thirty ships were now bottled up at Penang; like other ports in the region it was paralysed by fear of the *Emden.* One speedy, well-commanded vessel was stifling the maritime life of a continent. Brown, who had met von Müller and other German naval officers before the war, believed that the arrogance that was *de rigueur* with the Prussian army repelled the more sensitive type of man who wanted a service career, and instead these men chose the newly-formed German navy which had fewer constrictions in terms of personal attitudes.

Only the cooks were awake on the Russian ship at this early hour. At 300 metres the first torpedo was released, and raced toward the *Zemtchug.* It hit below the water line; there was a dull thud of an explosion and the old cruiser lifted slightly out of the water under the impact. But she was not sunk. The *Emden* then unleashed a dreadful barrage of gunfire upon the almost defenceless Russian ship — one of its gun crews managed to get to their weapon but their aim was wild, while the German shells were dead on target. The *Emden* manoeuvred into position to fire another torpedo. Pilot Brown, who was just coming into view of the action, saw the *Zemtchug* flare like magnesium and quickly disappear into the sea leaving only a yellow cloud of smoke behind. The *Sydney Morning Herald* printed the account of a Sydney man who was in Penang at the time. Rushing to the seafront he was in time to see a cruiser with four funnels emerging from the smoke: he thought it was the *Yarmouth* (it called there frequently) and then he was told (correctly) that the first torpedo from the German raider had disabled the electrical machinery for hoisting ammunition to the *Zemtchug's* guns. By now the *D'Iberville* was firing and von Müller could not stop to pick up survivors from the stricken Russian cruiser. The Sydney man joined two others on a small launch and went toward where the *Zemtchug* had sunk, leaving only her masts sticking above the surface of the water. He wrote:

The sea was strewn with dead fish, and wreckage, in addition to a large number of men swimming or clinging on to life-belts, planks, etc. We were the first out but some ships in the harbour had already lowered boats and were picking up the survivors. We rescued eighty-six men, and as other launches had then come up, turned back in order that the wounded might receive medical attention as quickly as possible. The spectacle was ghastly — men wounded all over with shrapnel bullets, pieces of shell, etc. Some had legs blown off ... the poor fellows displayed wonderful courage, although they must have been in fearful agony, and never whimpered. We tore our handkerchiefs, etc., up, and bandaged the men as well as we could.

The eighty-nine dead were laid in rows on the quay while the European women of the town rallied to nurse the injured sailors. Pilot Brown was ordered to head out and try to locate the patrol launch manned by members of the Straits Coast Defence Service, the *Sea Gull.* The Germans saw her first and thinking, in the heat of the moment, that it was a small torpedo boat, fired off a couple of shells, which fortunately caused no casualties. Out to sea, the British ship, the *Glenturret,* about to enter Penang with a cargo which included dynamite, was stopped by the German cruiser. At first, the boarding party told the British captain that his ship would be sunk and that he had ten minutes to lower the boats, but then a signal was made from the *Emden.* Lauterbach told the commander: 'I am ordered to ask you to convey to the authorities at Penang apologies for our firing on a small launch, which at first we took to be a torpedo boat. We hope no one was injured.' Von Müller, gallant though he was, had been told that the French destroyer, the *Mousquet,* was approaching, and there was no time to deal with the British freighter even had he wanted to do *so.*

It was simple folly on behalf of the French to take on the *Emden.* The *Mousquet* was blown out of the water within minutes, going down by the bow, the last sight of her being a momentary one of her stern lifting sharply into the air before sliding quickly beneath the sea. This time, the *Emden* had the time to stop and pick up the survivors who, the next day, were put on the steamer, the *Newburn,* stopped en route to Singapore with a cargo of salt. They were sent for medical treatment to a port at Sumatra across the narrow Straits of Malacca.

The *Newburn* was the German raider's last prize. Now von Müller decided to head for the Cocos Islands.

5

The Battle at Cocos Island

DIRECTION ISLAND, A PART of the Cocos group in the Indian Ocean, rises barely 150 centimetres above sea level. It had been leased by the Clunies-Ross family, which had a charter from Queen Victoria to manage the island group, to the Eastern Extension Telegraph Company. The company had built a cable relay station there, and from Cocos the submarine cables ran to Weltevreden, a suburb of Batavia (now Jakarta) in the Dutch East Indies, to Perth in Australia and to Rodriguez Island near Mauritius and thence to Africa. Its strategic importance in time of war was immense.

In operation, the interior of the Cocos cable station was, like that of a towering lighthouse, strangely quiet. All that could be heard was the low whirr of the relay motors, while the tape from the receivers would wind on to the floor in silence, with the roar of the breakers on the nearby shore the loudest sound as the machines relayed their tidings of gruesome battles on the Western Front to the newspaper readers of Adelaide, Brisbane, Dunedin and Wellington. The Cocos Islands themselves lay midway between Fremantle and Colombo and were by-passed by the mail steamers plying the Australian run; the only regular callers were the steamers sent every three months by the telegraph company although, before 1914 at least, one P&O skipper would regularly bring his ship close enough to Direction Island to lower barrels of fresh food and newspapers and books; these would be picked up by a boat sent out from the cable station. Most of the time, the staff of thirty led a drowsy existence. Except for occasional cyclones, the climate was extremely agreeable.

At 6 am on 9 November 1914 one of the staff members was just leaving the office after finishing his night duty when he was met by one of the Chinese workers who told him that there was a warship lying off the lagoon. It was, of course, the *Emden*, although it was not obvious to the staff right away. Von Müller's primary aim at Cocos was to disrupt British communications. He also hoped to harry shipping serving the West Australian ports and replicate the dislocation he had wrought in the Bay of Bengal when essential supplies were held in ports for fear of the German corsair. The raider's captain also believed his presence in that area would draw many of the British cruisers from the Indian Ocean, whereupon he would double back and make for Socotra Island (which lies off what is now Somalia but was then part of Britain's Aden Protectorate) and then cruise in the Gulf of Aden to prey on the ships plying between Suez and Bombay.

What von Müller did not know when he reached Cocos was that he had passed within eighty-eight kilometres of the huge convoy of troop ships carrying Australian and New Zealand soldiers under the protection of the *Sydney*, *Melbourne* and the Japanese battlecruiser *Ibuki*. The German ship could have run amok in the convoy, with rich pickings, had she been able to infiltrate at night (although her own demise would have surely ensued). The British heavy cruiser, the *Minotaur,* had started out with the troop convoy (one writer, seeing the convoy several weeks later in the Red Sea, described it as sailing two ships abreast in an immense string to the horizon and taking several hours to pass). On 8 November, the *Minotaur* had been detached and sent at full speed to South Africa in case the German East Asiatic Squadron made it around Cape Horn and headed for German South-West Africa.

The remaining ships in the British convoy had been enjoined to keep radio silence, and with some difficulty the Australian authorities had persuaded or prevented the country's newspapers from publishing full details of the convoy's make-up and sailing dates. On the night of 8 November, with the *Minotaur* gone, the convoy closed up and darkened ships. The *Melbourne* was leading with the *Sydney* and the *Ibuki* on the flanks. The ships steamed steadily to the north-east of the Cocos Island as unaware of the *Emden's* close proximity as the Germans were of theirs. Earlier that day, a Sunday, the German cruiser had met up with the collier *Exford* north of the island group and coaled from her. The *Emden* was by this time a sad sight, 'decks dusty from coal heaps, rusty bulkheads, scars and dents, a pigeon cote beside the funnel, one surviving pig tethered to a stanchion' as one description had it. Later the crew of the cruiser were treated to a large Sunday dinner from the recently captured chickens and fresh vegetables. After the meal, the crew was ordered to prepare for action the next morning. Everything that was not necessary was stowed and the men whiled away the rest of the evening smoking and singing. Those who were able to sleep did so as the engines continued their steady throb, the screws churning the water up as the *Emden* moved gradually closer to her target on Direction Island. At about half-past five, she dropped anchor at Port Refuge. The last act in the drama was about to be played.

HMAS Sydney [Australian War Memorial 301393]

The staff on Direction Island were not at first alarmed by the appearance of the warship. They had been in radio contact with the *Minotaur.* Von Müller had heard this communication although he did not know with whom it was being conducted. The land station had been sending out hourly transmissions in a three-figure code preceded with the word 'urgent' *en clair.* At first there was no reply, and the Germans believed it to be a general warning to passing traders. Then on the morning of 8 November the signals were acknowledged by an English warship using the call-letters 'NC' which von Müller supposed to be the light cruiser, the *Newcastle.* However, the ship using the signal 'NC' was clearly moving away from the area as the strength of the signal was gradually decreasing. When the wireless traffic finally ceased about noon, the *Emden's* wireless operators estimated the British ship to be more than 300 kilometres away. The coast, it seemed, was clear.

When members of the cable station staff climbed on to the roof to have a look at the ship — the ground itself being only slightly above sea level — they saw a warship flying no flag and with one funnel clearly made of canvas. The station's superintendent immediately ordered a distress signal to be sent. 'Strange ship in entrance' was soon being repeated with an 'SOS' signal added. At the same time a similar message was being sent out on the cables. Earlier several of the troopships had picked up a message 'Kativ Battav', which was the *Emden's* coded message to the *Buresk* to close up and join her ready for coaling. The operator at Cocos had signalled 'What is that code?', and received only jamming from the powerful Telefunken equipment on board the German cruiser, but the SOS signal, which was followed by 'SOS, *Emden* here' after they saw the dummy funnel appear to wobble, did get through the interference.

By this time most of the staff had been aroused from their beds just in time to see a steam launch towing two cutters heading for the shore. The task of disabling the station had been left to von Mücke with a party of about fifty men armed with machine guns, rifles and side arms, as well as enough equipment to quickly cause havoc. They were wearing tropical kit including the helmets issued for land operations in the tropics. Von Mücke had orders from his captain to destroy the cable and wireless stations and if possible to cut the cables (as the *Nurnberg* had done at Fanning Island); first the Australian cable, next the one to South Africa via Rodriguez Island, then that to the Dutch East Indies. He was to seize all code-books and records of messages and take them back to the *Emden*. Von Müller told von Mücke that, if the island was found to be garrisoned and ready to fight, the party should return to the ship and he would proceed to destroy the station by gun bombardment.

Once on shore, having seen that there would not be any resistance, von Mücke posted men to each of the buildings. The key operator was continuing to send messages — the last words that went down the cables were 'They are entering the door' — until he was found by the Germans and told to stop. The staff was assembled and placed under guard. The only weapons the staff possessed were a few twelve-bores and small arms and these were surrendered. Meanwhile, the German sailors were busy collecting all the papers from the wireless hut and bundling them up in the station's international code flags ready to be transported back to the *Emden*.

Then the demolition began. First came the sound of crashing glass, then the thud of axes slicing into wireless and cable equipment. What was opened by axe was then torn apart by hand, and when that was done, the tables and desks were overturned, spreading their debris across the floors. While all this was going on, another party of Germans was drilling holes in the base of the wireless mast in which to place dynamite. The station staff asked that it be made to fall clear of the tennis courts, which the Germans obliging did. The crew of the *Emden* laughed and joked as they saw the mast fall from their vantage point on the cruiser's deck.

The interior of the cable station after the German landing party had done its work. [Australian War Memorial EN396]

After the mast was dealt with, the landing party turned to the engine room, the switchboards, and even the seismograph, which was torn to pieces. The generator which powered the ice-making machine and the water condensing plant was saved only by the action of the Chinese greaser in charge of it; he pleaded with the Germans that it had nothing to do with the wireless station, so it was left intact.

The Germans began working on the cables with a handsaw, but this made little impression. Axes and files were brought to the job. They managed to cut the cable to Perth and then, to the amusement of the watching cable staff, spent a great deal of time sawing shore-ends which ran only a few hundred metres out to sea. In fact, the staff were treating the whole matter with good-humoured resignation. They were a great deal better humoured than were the invaders when told that German radio had broadcast news of several officers and men awarded the Iron Cross by the Kaiser. The Germans replied that they would have to be smothered in Iron Crosses in order to compensate them for what they had been through aboard the *Emden*. The piece of news that had really upset the sailors was that of the fall of Tsingtao to Japanese and British forces. They were a little cheered when the cable staff offered them tea with bread and jam.

The demolition work was abandoned when siren blasts from the cruiser recalled the landing party (by this time the *Emden,* having sighted the *Sydney,* was working up steam and preparing to get under way). The party was accompanied back to the jetty by members of the cable staff, the latter bringing their cameras along to record the scene. At 9.30 am the Germans pushed off with cheerful farewells to the staff, prematurely as it turned out. They would soon be back.

When the SOS was received from Cocos aboard the troop convoy ships, the commander in charge, Captain Mortimer Silver of the *HMAS Melbourne,* first intended to go for the German ship himself and ordered speed and a westward course, but then he swung back to the head of the convoy when he remembered that his prime responsibility was the safety of the troops. The Japanese were keen to do the job; upon receipt of the news, the *Ibuki* had hoisted all its battle flags and cleared for action, but the *Sydney* was on the side of the convoy closer to the Cocos Islands. The Australian ship (just a year old) could do at least three knots more than the 1907 Japanese battlecruiser, and the Australians probably felt that they wanted an Australian vessel to take the battle honours. The *Sydney,* under Captain John Glossop, was ordered to full speed and made for the islands.

The battle was uneven before it began: notwithstanding the *Emden's* reputation within the German Imperial Navy for the speed and accuracy of her gunnery, she was simply outgunned. Her 105-millimetre guns were no match for the *Sydney's* 150-millimetre armament. The *Emden's* gunnery work was to be a splendid example of discipline — she was able to fire a salvo at the Australian ship every six seconds which, when the Germans began shooting at a range of just under ten kilometres, meant that she had three separate salvoes in the air at one time. The other problem for the *Emden* was that while she could elevate her main guns to thirty degrees (which the British ships could not do), her shells were taking longer to reach the target than the *Sydney's.* The Australian warship, because of the larger calibre of her guns, could fire the same distance at a lower elevation. Furthermore, the *Sydney* had armour plating, thus making it less vulnerable when the *Emden* was firing at extreme range.

The *Sydney's* stokers did sterling work that morning, enabling the cruiser to surpass its maximum designed speed of 25.5 knots and, at one stage, she managed twenty-seven knots, smoke pouring from her stacks and most of the bow obscured by the huge wave of foam churned up as she punched through the waves at high speed. The Germans had seen her coming at about 9.00 am, although the lookout had at first presumed her to be the *Buresk*. Even the fact that the approaching vessel was giving off thick smoke — the collier normally gave off little smoke — did not alert the cruiser's officers because the *Buresk* had had a fire in her bunkers the previous day and it was assumed she was using partly-burned coal which would have explained the thick smoke. The situation was not helped by the lookout's report that the approaching vessel had two funnels. Then it slowly dawned — the masts were the height of a warship's. Von Müller cracked out the orders: 'Up anchor', 'Clear ship for action', 'Get steam up immediately to put on all possible speed.' The siren sounded to recall the landing party.

At 9.30 am the ship weighed anchor without retrieving the landing party. Prince Franz Joseph rushed to his action station in the torpedo flat and made a final test of the tube connections. As he did this he could feel the quivering of the ship as the engines strained to achieve full speed. On the bridge, von Müller thought he was about to face the *Newcastle* — given the 'NC' radio code the previous day — and did not discover the identity of his foe until after the battle was over. To what extent von Müller's actions were determined by this mistake can never be fully known; certainly the *Newcastle* would have been more of a match with only two 150-millimetre guns (to the *Sydney's* eight) and ten 105-millimetre guns. Regardless, von Müller knew he stood little chance of sinking the British ship; his main hope was to slow her down either by gunfire or by torpedo.

The battle lasted an hour and a half. Glossop's despatch to the Admiralty from Colombo six days later was a model of brevity:

… At 6.30 am on Monday, 9 November, a wireless message from Cocos was heard reporting that a foreign warship was off the entrance. I was ordered to raise steam for full speed at 7.00 am and proceed thither. I worked up to 20 knots, and at 9.15 am sighted land ahead and almost immediately the smoke of a ship, which proved to be *H.I.G.M.S. Emden* coming out towards me at a great rate. At 9.40 am fire was opened, she firing the first shot. I kept my distance as much as possible to obtain the advantage of my guns. Her fire was very accurate and rapid to begin with, but seemed to slacken very quickly, all casualties occurring in this ship almost immediately. First the foremast funnel of her went, secondly the foremast, and she was badly on fire aft, then the second funnel went, and lastly the third funnel, and I saw she was making for the beach on North Keeling Island, where she grounded at 11.20 am. I gave her two more broadsides and left her to pursue a merchant ship which had come up during the action.'

It was not until the next day that Glossop rendered assistance to the wounded on board the *Emden*. By that time the men had been without food or water all through the tropical day and night; some were driven to drinking salt water from the sea which drove them demented before they died. Those who saw the scenes aboard the German cruiser that next day, whether the witnesses were German or Australian, described them as some of the most horrifying they could ever imagine.

At the beginning of the battle, the *Emden* had scored the first hit. That first salvo hit the *Sydney's* after control section and wounded the sailors there, and then another shell hit the range-finder on the fore-upper bridge, killing the operator. It did not explode; had it done so it would almost certainly have killed Glossop and his other officers on the bridge. Another shell blew two holes in the steampipe beside the funnel and exploded behind the second starboard gun, killing two of the gun crew and wounding others. Some guncotton was ignited and flared up, giving the German gunners the momentary hope that they had hit some ammunition aboard the *Sydney*. The mess deck was wrecked by a shell, but no one was hurt.

By this time things were far worse aboard the *Emden*. The shells from the Australian cruiser with their lyddite — a high explosive consisting mainly of picric acid and suited to armour-piercing shells — had caused fires which were engulfing the Germans. The shells were smashing the German wireless, the steering gear (so that the ship had to be steered manually from the aft gear) and the voice-pipes by which the bridge communicated with the engine room. As the *Sydney's* broadsides hit home whole areas of decking buckled under the force of explosions below.

When von Müller ordered the hand-steering gear near the stern to be manned it was found that most of the men in that area of the ship had already been killed. Sailors from the forward signalling were ordered aft, but they found that the hand gear itself was jammed. From then on von Müller had to steer by the screws which, in the absence of voice-pipes, was a cumbersome business — a man had to run between the bridge and a hatch with each order to shout it below. The after guns were put out of action: one of the gun crews was blasted out of their emplacement into the ocean by the force of the explosions. Hans Harms, a twenty-two year old junior engineer, was in the starboard engine room. When a shell hit, only he and a warrant officer survived from the twenty men there; he crawled out on deck on the port side, and went to put his hands in his pockets only to realise that all his clothes had been blown from his body in the force of the blast. Shells were bursting everywhere around him, one of them throwing him over the side of the ship. Harms saved himself by grabbing a rope hanging from the mast, the mast itself by this time lying on the deck and protruding over the side of the ship. The gas from the lyddite shells had, in the meantime, forced Franz Joseph to abandon his torpedo flat. He and his men found the hatch through which they could escape was jammed because the coaming had been bent by explosions. They hurriedly unscrewed the hatch through which torpedoes were lowered from the deck. Once his own immediate danger had passed, Franz Joseph saw the extent of the chaos. Dead and wounded men were everywhere, the air full of groaning and plaintive cries for help:

> In the fore battery I found Oberleutnant Geerdes, who was wounded; he pointed out to me our gunnery officer, Gaede. Gaede was lying at the port gun breathing his last breath, dying fully conscious, for he still recognised me. His uniform was red with blood. He dozed while he was thanking me for the words of comfort I gave him, and was then carried on to the forecastle, where he soon afterwards closed his eyes for ever.

Smoke gushed from the hatches. Parts of the deck became white hot from the fires below and the surviving members of the crew were being forced forward as the fires spread from the stern. Von Müller had very little coal left. Two of the funnels were gone which meant that work was impaired below as the stokers fought smoke and fumes, and the engine room was on fire. Then the third funnel went as the *Sydney* closed range and continued to pump shells into the German raider. At one stage the Australian sailors cheered when the *Emden* disappeared into a pall of yellow smoke — only to re-emerge and continue firing defiantly at the *Sydney*.

It was nothing more than a gesture. Von Müller reported later that his remaining batteries were hard pressed to maintain fire because of the lack of ammunition and the serious casualties among gun crews and ammunition bearers. When his guns were finally silenced, von Müller swung away from the *Sydney* by stopping the starboard engine. As it was now impossible for the *Emden* to continue the fight, he decided to run aground on North Keeling Island in order to save the crew members who were still alive. Normally in a sea battle the defeated vessel would have sunk, taking all but the fittest survivors with it to the bottom. Shortly before grounding, von Müller ordered the engines stopped, then after impact he ordered them back to full speed again to jam the ship tightly on the rocks, followed by the order to draw all the fires in the boilers and flood the engine and boiler rooms. By this time, Glossop later estimated, the *Sydney's* shells had scored at least 100 hits on the *Emden*.

Now Glossop turned his attention to the *Buresk* which was making a run for it to the north-west. On board her were sixteen Germans, an English steward and a Norwegian cook, and eighteen Chinese crew members. Her crew had witnessed the damage inflicted on the *Emden* and, after a short chase, Glossop fired across her bow and hoisted the international code signal to stop. The German commander, Lieutenant-Commander Klopper, had no intention of allowing the *Buresk* to be re-taken by the British. He ordered the seacocks opened, and by the time the Australian sailors had boarded they realised it was impossible to save the collier. The crew was quickly taken off and the *Sydney's* guns pumped four shells into the *Buresk* to finish her off.

On the *Emden* von Müller had ordered that anyone who wanted to jump overboard and swim to shore was free to do so. Several men did; some were killed when waves dashed them on to the hard coral rock, while those who made it safely ashore found that there was no sign of water on North Keeling Island.

Von Müller also ordered the flooding of the magazines to avoid more fires and for the breech-blocks to be thrown overboard and the sights destroyed thereby rendering the guns unserviceable. The torpedo-director was also thrown overboard, and any surviving secret papers set alight. The wounded men who could be found had been brought to the forecastle where the ship's doctor tried to do what he could to treat the most badly wounded. What was left of the tablecloths and sheets was ripped up to add to the bandage supply. The assistant surgeon, having been thrown over-board earlier by one of the shell blasts, was found later in the day on the beach, dying after drinking salt water. The men still aboard the *Emden* were not much better off. The water tanks above the armoured deck had been shot away while those under the torpedo flat were by this time full of sea water. The small amount of drink-ing water left in the pipes was given to the most severely wounded of the men, but it did not go far, and their agony was exacerbated by the fact that sailcloth and other material used for awnings over the deck were stowed in compartments now under water and thus unreachable. There were no boats with which to evacuate the wounded: most of the boats were still with the landing party while the pinnace still aboard the raider was burned during the battle. Gulls attacked the prostrate men on the deck and had to be beaten off with cudgels and pistols.

The *Sydney,* whose damage was slight in terms of operation of the ship and with casualties of only three dead, one fatally wounded and eight wounded, now returned to the *Emden,* picking up some of the German ship's gunnery crew who had been struggling in the water for several hours. The Australian ship arrived off the *Emden* at about 4.00 pm on 9 November and Glossop saw that the German ensign was still flying, meaning technically that the *Emden* was still in the battle. Several histories have stoutly defended

Glossop for his subsequent action. He signalled to the *Emden* 'Will you surrender?', to which the German ship replied in morse 'What signal? No signal books'. Glossop then made to the *Emden,* this time in Morse; 'Do you surrender?', then 'Have you received my signal'? Von Müller said later that this signal was not understood, that his reply that he had no signal book was clearly indicative that he was prepared to negotiate, that his ship was plainly out of action and that Glossop should have sent a boat under a white flag. Instead, the *Sydney* recommenced firing at the helpless raider for five minutes, killing another twenty Germans, until the German ensign was hauled down and a white flag raised.

Glossop later justified his actions by stating that the captured Germans from the *Buresk* had been adamant that von Müller would never surrender and that he feared that the light cruiser the *Konigsberg* might have joined up with the *Emden* (it was actually still in East African waters) and that the *Emden* might still have been able to fire her guns. His story seems the less plausible of the two; there could have been no doubt in Glossop's mind that the German cruiser was high and dry and mortally damaged, and he could not have been unaware that von Müller had established a reputation for having gone to the most extraordinary lengths (when he had the whip hand) in order to avoid casualties.

The official history scorns von Müller's later accusation (made after he had spent some time with Glossop going over the battle) that the *Sydney's* captain, an able though not by any means an outstanding naval officer, had been egged on to this last salvo by his first officer. While the Australians were acting within the bounds of the conventions of naval warfare it appears that there was a considerable lack of imagination, not to mention humanity, on the bridge of the *Sydney* that afternoon.

The wrecked Emden *as seen from the decks of the* Sydney. [Australian War Memorial EN401]

The extensive damage can be seen clearly in this close-up of Emden [Author's collection]

Glossop then ordered the *Sydney* back to pick up two boat-loads of men from the *Buresk*. He stopped twice to pick up sailors from the sea, then headed for Direction Island, arriving there after dark and too late to discover what was going on at the cable station. While he waited, von Mücke and the rest of his landing party were quietly sailing away in a schooner, the *Ayesha,* which they had commandeered when they saw *Emden* under attack. It was then that Glossop turned his mind back to the plight of the *Emden,* taking the cable station's doctor to help his own medical team. An officer was sent over to the *Emden* to obtain von Müller's guarantee that, if the stricken Germans were taken aboard the *Sydney,* they would not interfere with the operations of the Australian cruiser while they were aboard. For four hours on the afternoon of 10 November the wounded were transhipped. The operation was resumed at 5.00 am on 11 November. At Colombo, Glossop later described the sight of the *Emden* to war correspondent A.B. 'Banjo' Paterson:

> Everybody on board was demented — that's all you could call it, just fairly demented — by shock, and fumes, and the roar of shells bursting among them … One of our shells had landed behind a gun shield, and had blown the whole gun-crew into one pulp. You couldn't even tell how many men there had been.

In his official report to the Admiralty, Glossop limited himself to the term 'indescribable' to explain the conditions aboard the *Emden.* When Franz Joseph went to find his friend Oberleutant von Levetzow all he found was an unrecognisable body, which he identified as his friend's from the shape of the head and the star of rank on the jacket. During the night several of the wounded had died. When the remainder of the wounded were finally taken aboard the *Sydney*, the ship's two doctors and the one from the cable station operated for ten hours without a break on the worst cases. The surviving doctor from the *Emden*, Dr Luther, was incapable of helping after the emotional trauma of those hours of nightmare. The list of the *Emden's* dead was: killed, drowned or died of wounds — 134 men, consisting of seven officers, one pay-master, four warrant officers, twenty-five petty officers, ninety-two ordinary seamen, one civilian cook, one barber and three Chinese laundrymen. Seriously wounded were one warrant officer, three petty officers, seventeen ordinary seamen; lightly wounded were two officers, two warrant officers, nine petty officers and thirty-one ordinary seaman. The unhurt totalled six officers (including von Müller and Franz Joseph), five warrant officers, thirty-nine petty officers and sixty-seven ordinary seamen.

Whatever one may think of some of Glossop's actions, he had the grace to signal ahead to Colombo that, because he would be arriving with many badly wounded Germans laid out on his decks, he wanted no cheering from other ships when the *Sydney* entered harbour. His wishes were respected, and the cruiser steamed up the harbour in almost total silence. A small number of the crew of the *Emden* were sent to prisoner of war camps in Australia, but the bulk, including von Müller, were imprisoned on Malta.

The *HMS Cadmus,* a gunboat of the China squadron, was allotted the task of going to the *Emden* wreck and disposing of all the bodies still on board and burying all the Germans left lying on the shore at North Keeling Island. It was a dreadful assignment; by the time the ship arrived all the human remains were putrid from decomposition.

A visitor to the site on the first anniversary of the battle reported in *Life* magazine that bleached bones and skulls could still be detected lying in the shallows; the photographs which accompanied the article show that a year later the forward section of the *Emden* was still remarkably intact, but that she was broken amidships and that the stern, which had taken the worst punishment in action, had totally disintegrated. The Australian Government called for tenders for disposal of the wreck. In July 1915 the Department of Defence accepted the tender of a group of Sydney men who were planning to bring the *Emden* to Sydney and place her on show; they proposed to plug the holes in the hull with concrete, remove the smashed superstructure, move a suction pump in to get rid of the water in the hull and then tow her off with the powerful tug they planned to hire. There was no reason, members of the syndicate vowed, why she should not then float off the reef. The amazing scheme then allowed for the *Emden* to be towed to the nearest port and, after makeshift repairs, sail to Sydney under her own steam. It was planned to have the German raider at Farm Cove by Christmas. In October, the Navy announced that the deal was off, that it would undertake the salvage of the *Emden* itself. A gunboat with 'all the necessary equipment' and crewed with divers and engineers would leave in a fortnight, the announcement promised. However, the gunboat — *HMAS Protector* — radioed backed to its base in mid-November that the German ship was a total wreck and that the huge breakers which continuously swept over the remnants made salvage impossible.

On 11 January 1916, the Minister of the Navy, Mr Jensen, announced: 'It may now be considered as certain that nothing more can be done towards salving either the remains of the Emden, or any trophies from her, except such as may be cast ashore.' A visitor to the Cocos group in 1919 reported that almost all traces of the Emden had disappeared.

6

Von Mücke's Escape

THE GERMAN LANDING PARTY HAD, with their steam launch and two cutters in tow, tried to follow the *Emden* when the cruiser put to sea to meet the approaching British warship. It soon became clear that the raider was working up to full speed as quickly as possible, and that the landing party would be left behind. Von Mücke had no choice other than to turn back to Direction Island. The Germans had already noticed a little white schooner anchored nearby; their first instinct had been to sink her, but the urgent summons from the *Emden,* together with the unexpectedly long time it had taken to cut the cables, had meant that the Germans had quite forgotten about the *Ayesha.*

The ninety-nine ton schooner derived its name from the favourite wife of the Prophet Mohammed, and she was depicted in the figurehead. She was owned by the Clunies-Ross family — as were the entire group of islands — and had been employed to run between the group and Batavia two or three times a year, carrying copra out and returning with provisions and supplies from the

Dutch East Indies. She was less than ten years old, but was not in the best seaworthy condition and, as von Mücke was to discover, she did not handle well in the open sea. The *Ayesha* was idle on 9 November, having been supplanted by a steamship service to the Cocos group. On board her that morning were the captain, Mr J. E. Partridge, and two sons of the island's patriarch, Cosmo and Edmund Clunies-Ross. According to an account given by Partridge on his return to London, those aboard the schooner were given twenty minutes to get ashore; the captain left wearing his white suit and carrying his navigating equipment.

The Ayesha

Being possessed of a German flag, the *Emden's* lieutenant then proclaimed German possession of the island and proclaimed martial law. He knew, however, that he would have to escape quickly because it would not be long before the British came back. The Germans had watched the pummelling of their ship from the roof of the wireless station. The Germans had four machine-guns, twenty-four rifles, and some side arms.

There was no alternative but to commandeer the *Ayesha*. Von Mücke asked the superintendent about the provisions stored on the island. When told there was enough for four months for the staff, the German said he would take two months' worth and that he would return them if he were able at the first port of call. He assured himself of the correct address of the company in Singapore and would wire them that the cable station staff had been left destitute and needed supplies.

Although there were attempts later to play down the friendly atmosphere which developed that day — from British accounts — there seems little doubt that the cable staff felt quite safe and relaxed with the Germans and, apart from hiding some transmission and electrical equipment from the landing party, did not make any undue difficulties for the landing party. For his part, von Mücke was quite agreeable to allowing the cable staff to make a run for it should the British ship come back before the *Ayesha* was ready to leave and the Germans were forced to make a last ditch stand. The superintendent of the station, Darcy Farrant, wanted both to protect his own men, and to prevent circumstances under which the British ship would be reluctant to attack for fear of civilian casualties (the term 'British' being used here because at this stage nobody knew it was the *Sydney* involved in the battle). In fact, the cable staff helped the Germans to assemble the provisions they needed. One of the Germans wanted to write a letter to his mother, and so he was taken to a room and given pen and paper. The station staff fraternised with their captors — like their predecessors aboard the dredge headed for Tasmania, they had few diversions and this was certainly a day they would all remember. The staff handed out liberal supplies of beer to the toiling Germans, and turned on sandwiches and cigarettes too. The Germans obviously welcomed the chance to talk about themselves, and those who were not actively engaged in loading the schooner sat on the wireless station roof with the British, smoking and talking about the fight they had been watching out to sea. Von Mücke requisitioned nearly seven hundred litres of water, while his request for clothes met a ready response; his men had landed on the island in thin tropical uniforms and they had been told to wear old uniforms because they would be doing heavy work. So they were now rigged out in a strange mixture of civilian clothes. Von Mücke stated rather ungraciously in his memoir of the escape that most of the clothes were too small for his men, but photographs of the day show no noticeable disparity between the size of the landing party and their captives. The amiable atmosphere was capped by three rousing cheers from both the boats and the jetty as the Germans moved off toward the *Ayesha*.

The Germans help themselves to stores from the wireless station
[Australian War Memorial]

The Germans have clambered into their boats and the steam pinnace is about to pull them out to Ayesha *sitting off the island.* [Australian War Memorial EN395]

Once the Germans had gone, and the cable staff set about restoring communication with the outside world. That night they dug out some old oil lamps which provided light in the absence of electricity; there were also spare parts and equipment which had remained undiscovered by the Germans. They could not get through to either Perth or Rodriguez Island, but did manage at last to raise Singapore to whom they gave a brief account of the day's happenings and then, leaving the debris until the morning, turned in after an exhausting day. The next morning more undamaged equipment was found, and contact with Rodriguez resumed. That next day also brought the *Sydney* back to Direction Island and it was only then the cable staff found out the true identity of the vessel. The Australians sent a cutter ashore for the island's doctor and for medical supplies.

Aboard the *Ayesha,* von Mücke made a short speech to his crew and then called for three cheers for the Kaiser. The steam launch was attached by a stout rope to the bow of the schooner and was ordered to tow *Ayesha* out of the lagoon. The schooner had no charts for the island and there was a very real chance she would strike the coral which, given the state of the hull, could have ended the great adventure there and then. The tropical darkness fell quickly, von Mücke's luck held, and as the schooner successfully negotiated the lagoon entrance, the crew from the steam launch were recalled. The launch was cut loose and sent chugging off into the night while the crew set their sails.

It was soon clear that this was not going to be a pleasure cruise. The *Ayesha* had been designed for a crew of five plus the captain, so that most of von Mücke's men had to sleep in the hold, a spare sail being spread over the iron ballast. After a few nights of this, the men set about making hammocks from rope and sailcloth. These offset some of the discomfort from the schooner's violent motion. There were two small cabins aft, but these were declared uninhabitable due to swarms of cockroaches. Von Mücke and his two lieutenants allotted to themselves the small deckhouse which had two beds, but at least one of the three men was on duty at any one time. The tiny stove in the galley was patently inadequate for the fifty Germans. So, some of the iron ballast was used to build a larger crude stove in which an open fire burned while the men suspended pots over it on rods. All cooking was done with salt water, most of the meals being rice cooked with smoked sausage, corned beef or some tinned food, served with tea or coffee. The crew had to eat in relays, there being insufficient plates and utensils. Unfortunately, the water tanks were dirty and the water commandeered at Cocos was found to be fouled. There were some bottles of seltzer water, but von Mücke decided that these should be kept for emergencies.

Rain started to fall on 13 November. The men had already cleaned out the water tanks and a large sail with a hole in the middle was stretched out over a funnel which brought the water down into the tanks. Soon the tanks were full, as was every bucket, can and other container on the ship. By adding a little lime juice the water became very palatable. For washing, an ingenious 'swinging bath' was devised: the scuppers on both sides of the deck were blocked up, so trapping the rainwater; the men then lay on the deck and as the ship rolled the water swished from one side to the other. The two jolly boats were also allowed to fill with water.

A large portion of the landing party had been made up of men who had never been on a sailing ship before, so von Mücke had to identify which men knew something of ship handling. Others were set to patch and mend the rotten sails or to fix the pumps (which were not working) so that the water — which threatened to rise to the men's sleeping level in the hold — could be pumped out and the ship dried. The decks were swabbed with sea water. In spare moments, the sailors would teach others some of the basic principles of sailing, or they would sleep or play with the few packs of cards which had been taken from Direction Island. A few men tried to catch fish (without any luck). At night they would gather on the deck to sing. There were some frightening moments when storms broke, and all the sails had to be furled to save them from tearing. At one stage smoke was seen on the horizon, but the Germans were not detected: they were becalmed and all the sails had been furled.

Their target was Padang in Sumatra — more than 1,100 kilometres from Cocos. As land was sighted on 23 November, von Mücke 'cleared for action'; he was prepared to come into contact with English or Japanese torpedo-boat destroyers. There would be no surrender. The Germans planned, if such a ship came on the scene, to tack in front of it and wait until the other vessel came alongside and then grapple with it at close quarters. Four holes were cut in the schooner's rail to allow the machine-guns a clear field of fire. That evening the *Ayesha* stood off the coast of Sumatra and, as von Mücke had no charts, he did not want to negotiate the Seaflower Channel to Padang at night. The captain handed out a bottle of seltzer water to each man as a special treat. Their tobacco had already run out and the hardier members of the crew had taken to smoking tea leaves.

The next day von Mücke could see the islands and reefs which dotted the channel, but the wind was blowing the *Ayesha* out to sea. The only solution was to lower the jolly boats and tow the schooner in the right direction. Rowing hard in an open boat fully exposed to the tropical sun was highly unpleasant for the men picked for the job, although they got some help when the oars of the *Emden's* cutters were tied together in pairs and men rowed from the deck of the *Ayesha.*

A warship was seen lying to. Then, as von Mücke recorded:

Suddenly, the ship that had been lying so motionless began to move. Thick clouds of smoke poured from the smokestacks; she turned sharply, headed for us, and approached at high speed. In a short time we recognised the ensign of the Netherlands flying at the mast-head .... There was no reason for us to show our colours. We therefore quickly gathered up all our rifles, and stowed them, together with our artillery equipment, away below decks. All the men quickly disappeared down the main hatchway, which was closed after them.

Only von Mücke and one other sailor stayed on deck and from their tatty clothing could never have been taken for members of the German Imperial Navy. The visitor was the Dutch destroyer *Lynx,* and she slowed to pass the *Ayesha* at a distance of about fifty metres. Von Mücke could see all the Dutch officers on the bridge were studying his ship through binoculars. As the *Lynx* passed astern their glasses were turned on the place where the *Ayesha's* name had been covered by a thick coat of white paint. After following for a while, the destroyer made off in the direction of Padang, only to reappear that evening as the schooner neared Padang, and the destroyer proceeded to follow the *Ayesha* at the speed of one knot (the schooner's maximum speed in the light breeze). Von Mücke decided to take the initiative; using a bull's-eye lantern and holding a board in front to produce Morse signals, he made to the *Lynx* 'Why are you following me?'. The Dutch vessel acknowledged the signal, but gave no answer to the question. He repeated the signal, only to get the same reply.

On the morning of 27 November the *Ayesha* at last managed to enter Dutch territorial waters, upon which von Mücke ordered the ensign and colours to be raised. At noon, a Malay pilot came aboard and — quite content with the promise of later payment from the German consul in Padang — agreed to take the sailing vessel through the channel and its dangerous reefs. Soon after, the *Lynx* once again drew close and von Mücke ordered the customary salute between warships. His entire crew stood at attention on deck and the officers saluted, the Dutch at once returning the salute.

'I am sending a boat', the Germans signalled, and von Mücke donned his best clothes to visit the Dutch ship. Once aboard, von Mücke explained who he was and was assured the *Lynx* would not prevent them entering harbour but it was likely they would not be allowed to leave. On dropping anchor, the *Ayesha* was soon surrounded by boats from the German merchantmen in the harbour (the *Kleist,* the *Rheinland* and the Norddeutcher-Lloyd cargo ship the *Choising),* as well as one from an Austrian freighter.

The merchant seamen, although they were not allowed on board in case it harmed von Mücke's case with the Dutch authorities, passed them cigars, cigarettes, tobacco, watches, clothing, books, letters and — most treasured — German newspapers. While the papers were nearly two months old, they were an antidote to the sole diet of captured English papers the Germans had been reading, and the news was slanted somewhat more favourably to the Kaiser's war effort.

The Dutch wanted to make the *Ayesha* a prize of war. They were encouraged in their stand by the Belgian-born harbour master who had rather strong feelings about the Germans, and the Dutch were reluctant to antagonise the Japanese and British. The Germans argued that *Ayesha* was a commissioned warship, and that she should be allowed the legal twenty-four hours to take on necessary provisions. Von Mücke needed water, food, sailcloth, clothing, nautical charts and soap, toothbrushes (of which they had none), hair brushes and shoe polish. The Dutch replied that they were forbidden under neutrality rules to supply charts, and that even soap and toothpaste would increase the *Ayesha's* 'war strength'. The Germans decided they could endure not cleaning their teeth and to make do with one comb for the whole crew, nor would they be deterred by Dutch warnings that they could not hope to avoid capture by either Japanese or British warships.

The Dutch, convinced that the Germans planned to take their chances at sea, changed their minds and gave von Mücke some supplies. Before the twenty-four hour deadline approached, the *Ayesha* was towed toward the harbour entrance, and her sails unfurled. Von Mücke had, meanwhile, taken the precaution of handing the German Consul a rendezvous point should any of the merchant ships be able to meet him at sea. Just after the *Ayesha* passed out of Dutch territorial waters, a small boat came alongside with two naval reserve men from the *Rheinland*.

Now they were fifty-two.

Two British ships passed within sight of the slow-moving Germans as they sailed up the coast of Sumatra. The first ship made no sign of noticing her, but the second — a merchant ship which von Mücke feared might be armed as an auxiliary cruiser — showed a great deal more interest. To allay her curiosity, von Mücke signalled 'Please give me the geographical position' which was a common request from sailing ships to steamers. The information was supplied, with the question 'Who are you?' The Germans quickly grabbed the four closest signal flags, knotted two of them so that they could not be read, then hoisted them on the main mast where they would be partly obscured by sail. The British ship was apparently satisfied, although as it was pulling away it signalled that it could not understand the identification; no doubt the deception was considered incompetence on the part of some native crew.

On 14 December the *Choising* appeared. She was greeted by the crew of the *Ayesha,* many of them in the rigging and most of them naked or semi-naked. A tempest broke that night which prevented the ships from closing and during which a loud crack announced the loss of all of the forward sail. After some hair-raising moments, it was possible, on 16 December, for the *Ayesha* to be taken in tow. The supplies were transhipped, along with the figure-head and the steering wheel as mementoes. The *Ayesha* was now of no further use, and holes were drilled in her hull. The whole crew stood on the stern of the *Choising* to watch the schooner's end. She had been their home for a month and a half and they had travelled 1,709 nautical miles. Gradually the schooner sank lower and lower in the water, then a shudder went right through the ship. There was a pause after which the iron ballast rolled forward, sending the stern up into the air, upon which the *Ayesha* shot suddenly below the waves.

As far as speed was concerned, the Germans were not much better off aboard the *Choising*. Von Mücke, being a naval officer, was now in command, and found that her best speed was seven and a half knots. Her poor coal, and most of that partly lost in a bunker fire, meant her speed was down to about four knots. He considered the alternatives: Tsingtao had been captured; they also entertained the notion of joining the *Konigsberg* off East Africa, but they did not know where she was. They had still not learned that the *Konigsberg* was bottled up on Rufigi River in German East Africa by British warships, nor did they know that there had been considerable fighting between the German and British colonies in East Africa. The last and only viable choice was to try to make it home and rejoin the fight.

The discovery, from a newspaper on board the collier, that Turkey had joined the war on Germany's side clinched the matter. Von Mücke decided he would sail into the Red Sea and make for Turkish territory (in what is now Saudi Arabia). To aid their safe passage, the *Choising* was disguised as a Genoa-registered Italian (and therefore neutral) ship, the *Shenir*. A green curtain served as the basis for an Italian flag, with other coloured material sewn on and the Italian coat of arms was painted onto the white strip. They also sailed south of the normal steamer routes to avoid contact with British ships plying between Aden and the Indian ports.

On 7 January 1915, the Germans sighted the Straits of Perim at the narrow point between Aden (now Yemen) and Djibouti which opens on to the Red Sea. Von Mücke knew that if they were caught at this vital stage the *Choising*, given its fuel problems, could not make a run for it and it would be impossible to evade any ship which set out in pursuit. He ordered the longboats swung out so that — if intercepted — he could beach the collier and use the longboats to get ashore, where he would cause as much trouble as he could in British Somaliland. The long boats were equipped with water, food and ammunition. The straits, now known as Bab-el-Mandeb, were very narrow and the German ship hugged the African coast, a darkened vessel against a dark background. The major threat was the huge light operated by the British on the island of Perim, which did catch the *Choising* in its rays briefly while no one at Perim was looking. The Germans saw two English warships lying near Perim exchanging lamp signals in Morse, but they were obviously too busy to notice the collier painfully inching its way along the coast. After two hours of high tension, the Germans were safely in the Red Sea.

The next day, 8 January, the *Choising* was closing on Hodeida, believed to be held by the Turks (in what is now Yemen). Von Mücke believed there to be a railway from the port running either inland or northwards. At night, the Germans saw a row of lights they assumed were on a dock. Von Mücke took most of his men with him in the longboats and instructed the skipper of the collier to return and watch for his signals at specified times, one of which would be to run for shelter to Massawa on the African coast in neutral Italian Eritrea. It was just as well they were cautious; the lights on the 'dock' turned out to be the French armoured cruiser *Desaix*.

The Germans had landed about thirty kilometres from Hodeida and were soon engaged by about a hundred Bedouin tribesmen. A party of Arabs came out and parley would have begun, except that there was no common language, until one of von Mücke's party produced a gold coin with the Kaiser's head upon it. At last, comprehension. The Arabs knew that 'aleman' was an ally of their Turkish masters. Then a detachment of Turkish soldiers arrived to escort the party to Hodeida. Von Mücke reported that they were greeted in the town by flag-waving and cheering crowds. They were given food and clean clothes — and the news that there was no railway. At the appointed time, the signal was given to the *Choising* to sail for internment at Massawa.

Despite the generous hospitality, the sailors did not adjust to the climate or the food. The combination of hot days, cold nights, and bad water soon brought on serious outbreaks of dysentery and malaria. Von Mücke decided, based upon what he had been told by the Turks, that they would be a lot better off at the Yemeni capital of Sana'a where the mountain air would restore the health of his men. To cheers for the Sultan and the Kaiser and to a band playing *Deutschland, Deutschland Uber Alles* his men wound out of Hodeida aboard an uncomfortable caravan of horses, mules and donkeys. They could travel across the desert only at night.

Sana'a proved to be just as calamitous as Hodeida. So cold was it that most of the sailors developed some sort of fever, cramps or bad colds. To make matters worse, von Mücke found he could proceed no further up the Arabian peninsula. There was nothing for it but to return to Hodeida. It was quite clear that the Turks had failed to live up to the role normally expected of allies. The only positive reward from the Sana'a episode was that the Turkish commander there took the trouble to advise his government in Constantinople of von Mücke's arrival. The news was passed on to Berlin, and eventually the information was published world-wide. Before that, the fate of the fifty men after leaving Padang had been a mystery.

Von Mücke decided to take to the water again. Having sent the *Choising* away, he now had to resort to two *zambucks*, Arab dhow-like craft, to continue his journey up the coast. One of them sank, which meant all the men now had to be accommodated on one boat at the expense of their supplies which were jettisoned in order to keep the *zambuck* afloat. Four days later they reached Al Qunfidhah where they were fed well by Turkish authorities.

Then their hopes were dashed once again. The port of Jeddah was blockaded by the British. The sailors once more took to the land. Having left their boat at Al Lith, the Germans mounted camels for an inland route to Jeddah. On the fourth day, 31 March 1915, they suddenly came under fire. The Germans pulled their camels down and returned the fire with their machine guns which were particularly effective. This was followed up by a bayonet charge (the sailors having all clipped on their bayonets as soon as the firing started and without any order to do so). The Arabs, obviously startled by the unfamiliar tactics, retreated. By daylight von Mücke could determine that there were at least three hundred Bedouin and that some bold strategy was needed to get them out of trouble. One of his men was dead, another had been badly wounded.

Eventually the Arabs made their terms known: they wanted £11,000 and all the camels, arms, water and ammunition that the Germans had; in return for which they would let the party go. Von Mücke had no illusions about how far they would get if they agreed to those terms. All the next day the Germans dug in and waited.

Even their most trying experiences so far had not prepared the men from the *Emden* for this. The dead camels were starting to smell and had to be carried away from the trenches, the sun was blisteringly hot and the sand got into everything. Some of the men assigned by the Turks to accompany the party had fled, and von Mücke decided to send his last two Arabs to Jeddah for help.

By the morning of 3 April it looked as if the game was up. The water, already severely rationed, would all be gone by the end of that day. Negotiations re-opened with the Bedouin, and then von Mücke heard shots from the distance. The Bedouin melted away, and the Germans were left silently wondering what had happened. Eventually a column of Arab troops arrived, led by a man who introduced himself as the representative of the Emir of Mecca who had heard of the attack and ordered the rescue of the Germans. Von Mücke, by this time thoroughly wary (and weary) of Levantine duplicity and treachery, suspected another trap. His suspicions eased somewhat when Prince Abdullah, second son of the Emir, arrived on the scene. The next day they rode into Jeddah.

From there on, the journey was arduous but, by comparison with what they had endured, relatively uneventful. Another *zambuck* was hired and the surviving Germans sailed up the coast, anchoring each night, until they reached Al Wajh, where they once again boarded camels to travel inland to the railway at Al Ula. The German government had arranged special trains. The train trip to Constantinople lasted seventeen days, much of the time spent feting with the local people along the line. The trains themselves had been well stocked with food, brandy and champagne. They had arrived in Al Ula, in effect the end of their adventure, on 7 May, two days short of six months since they had set out from Direction Island. At Aleppo in Syria, the original landing party found two full mailbags of letters from home, cigars, chocolate, iron crosses handed out as liberally as ever by the Kaiser, and new uniforms.

On the afternoon of 23 May 1915, at Haidar Pasha railway station — the end of the line to Constantinople — the Germans stepped down from the train and back into the service of the

German Imperial Navy. Admiral Souchon, head of the Navy's Mediterranean division, stood on the platform as von Mücke formed his men into ranks, and then announced that the landing party from the *SMS Emden* of five officers, seven petty officers and thirty men were reporting for duty.

7

The Cruise of the *Wolf*

A model of the Wolf *showing the flaps which, when raised, hid the guns. The heights of the masts and funnel could be adjusted to alter the raider's appearance and profile.* [Paul Schmalenbach Collection]

THE CRUISE OF THE raider *Wolf* began on 30 November 1916 and ended — back where it began, at Kiel — fifteen months later, on 24 February 1918. In that time she steamed more than 100,000 kilometres and, what was most remarkable, the *Wolf's* presence was often not suspected even after ships mysteriously failed to arrive at their destinations on time. She mined the coasts of Malaya, South Africa, Australia and New Zealand with impunity, and in her cruise sank nearly 140,000 tons of shipping, ranging from fast mail steamers to aged sailing vessels.

It is necessary to digress here and look at the entire German raider campaign in order to assess the value of the *Wolf* in the war at sea. The *Emden*, one can say, certainly did prove a great irritation to British; not only did she tie up warships in the hunt for her, but delayed troop movements from India, Australia and New Zealand and prevented the shipping of cargoes for the British war machine.

Of the other raiders, the *Karlsruhe* was in the West Indies at the outbreak of war and raided off the South American coast for three months, sinking seventeen merchant ships and was heading northwards to bombard the British port of Barbados when — in what is believed to be spontaneous combustion in the ammunition — she was ripped in two by a gigantic explosion; 260 German sailors were killed as a result. The cruiser, *Dresden*, was also in the West Indies and, in orders sent from Berlin just a few days before war began, she was instructed to ignore earlier orders to make a dash for Germany. and instead to conduct raider warfare. Incidentally, one German historian, Heinz Hohne, has written that Germany was now paying dearly for the fact that her 'battleship-crazy admirals' had neglected cruiser construction for many years and that only second-rate ships like the *Dresden* (and the *Emden* for that matter) had been assigned to foreign service and too few supply ships had been provided to keep these cruisers fully operational.

The *Dresden* set course south to operate near Cape Horn but did not pause in the South Atlantic to target British ships using Argentine ports. Instead she passed around the Cape and joined von Spee's forces which were heading for the coast of

Chile. The East Asiatic Squadron had, initially, made little impact apart from causing the British to wonder where it was; had von Spee disbanded the squadron, which was too small in firepower for a major naval engagement against a British fleet anyway, and left each warship to engage in raider warfare like the *Emden*, the effect on Allied shipping in the Indian and Pacific Oceans might have been immense.

Instead von Spee fatefully left Valparaiso and steamed around Cape Horn to its doom by running into a vastly superior British force off the Falkland Islands on 8 December 1914; his plan had been to destroying the British wireless station there.

He was no doubt encouraged by his first encounter with the British off the Chilean city of Coronel. Rear-Admiral Sir Christopher Cradock, aboard the armoured cruiser *Good Hope*, had with him the warships *Monmouth* and *Glasgow* along with the armed merchant cruiser *Otranto*. Cradock was charged with finding the Germans. *Good Hope* was crewed largely by green reservists and cadets, and the experience of the men manning *Monmouth* was not much greater.

On 1 November 1914 *Glasgow* sighted smoke. It turned out the approaching ship was *Leipzig*. With light fading, Cradock was worried he could lose the Germans at night so began his attack at 7.30 pm even though visibility for him was poor; the Germans had an advantage because the British ships were silhouetted against the setting sun. The experience of the German gun crews also showed, with *Good Hope* and *Monmouth* being hit more than thirty times. The fate of the battle was sealed when, at 7.50 pm, the magazine exploded on *Good Hope* and the cruiser went down with all hands. Nor were there any survivors aboard *Monmouth*, which was already on fire when *Nürnberg* got to point blank range and pumped shell after shell into the British warship until she went down. Nearly 1,600 British sailors died that day.

The Germans had only another five weeks to savour their victory before the British exacted revenge off the Falklands.

The armoured cruiser Gneisenau [Paul Schmalenbach Collection]

SMS Scharnhorst *showing her paces.* [Paul Schmalenbach Collection]

In his dispatch to the Admiralty after he had destroyed the German fleet off the Falklands, Vice Admiral Sir Frederick Doveton-Sturdee said his squadron arrived at the Port Stanley, Falkland Islands, on the morning of 7 December to take on coal before resuming the search for the enemy ships. The battle cruiser *HMS Invincible* was flying his flag, and was accompanied by another battle cruiser *Inflexible*, the armoured cruisers *Carnarvon* (with Rear Admiral Archibald Soddart on board), *Kent* and *Cornwall*, the light cruisers *Glasgow* and *Bristol* and the armed merchantman *Macedonia*. There was also the old and very slow battleship *Canopus* which had been run into a mud bank and stationed at the entrance to the harbour with guns pointing to sea.

A column of smoke was spotted just after 8.00 am the next day. By 9.20, the *Gneisenau* and *Nürnberg* came within range of *Canopus* and the British ship opened fire. The German ships increased power and headed toward the rest of their squadron.

At 12.20 pm, after several hours of pursuit, Doveton-Sturdee decided to attack with the two battle cruisers and *Glasgow*, the *Inflexible* opening fire at 12.55 pm. The battle cruisers concentrated their fire on *Scharnhorst* and *Gneisenau*; by 3.00 pm there was a fire forward on *Scharnhorst* and 'her fire slackened perceptibly' (as Doveton-Sturdee noted in his subsequent report) and soon her third funnel had been shot away. The other German ship had been damaged badly by shells from *Inflexible*.

Doveton-Sturdee continued: 'At 4.04 pm the *Scharnhorst*, whose flag remained flying to the last, suddenly listed heavily to port, and within a minute it became clear she was a doomed ship, for the list increased very rapidly until she lay on her beam ends, and at 4.17 pm she disappeared'. The *Gneisenau*, meanwhile, was badly damaged but managed to land one shell on *Invincible*. 'At 6.00 pm the *Gneisenau* heeled over very suddenly, showing the men gathered on her decks and then walking on her sides she lay for a minute on her beam ends before sinking', the report to the Admiralty continued. Many of the approximately two hundred men who ended up in the water succumbed to the very cold water and drowned. The *Invincible* rescued 108 men, fourteen of whom were found to be dead after being brought on board.

While the two big German ships had turned to port and attracted the attention of the British battle cruisers, the light cruisers turned to starboard to make good their escape. The *Dresden* was leading with *Nürnberg* and *Leipzig* on each flank. The *Glasgow*, *Cornwall* and *Kent* immediately set off in pursuit while the slower *Carnarvon* stayed with the battle cruisers.

The *Leipzig* caught fire at 7.17 pm, three hours after the British cruisers began firing, then by 9.00 pm had rolled on to her port side and disappeared. Meanwhile, the *Nürnberg* was on fire and had ceased firing by 6.35 pm; after another round from Kent, the German cruiser hauled down her battle flags. The *Nürnberg* sank at 7.27 pm, with only seven men surviving.

While these German ships were being pursued, the *Dresden* used her superior speed to escape, helped by the sky becoming overcast and so reducing visibility.

In all, about 2,200 Germans died that day compared to eighteen Royal Navy deaths. The British ships had fired a total of 1,174 large calibre (twelve inch, 13.5 inch, fourteen inch and fifteen inch) shells.

The *Dresden* fled back around the Cape into the Pacific and hid at Tierra del Fuego until being ordered out of territorial waters by a Chilean destroyer. On 27 February *Dresden* caught and sank a British sailing vessel, the *Conway Castle* but the Germans' coal was almost exhausted. Then *Dresden* sailed into a harbour at the Juan Fernandez Islands and the captain asked the Chileans to intern the ship and crew. On 14 March *Glasgow*, in breach of Chile's neutrality, shelled the immobilised *Dresden*. The Germans were forced to scuttle their ship.

Germany's naval power outside Europe, such as it was, now had to rely on the armed merchant cruisers. In East Africa, as already noted, the *Konigsberg* had been effectively put out of action by British forces. The other raiders of the early war had been equipped hurriedly for the task. The *Prinz Eitel Friedrich* failed in her appointed task of raiding off the West Australian coast through lack of coal while, in the South Atlantic, the converted passenger liner *Cap Trafalgar*, flagship of the Hamburg South America Line (and on her maiden voyage in Buenos Aires when war began), was sunk by a similarly converted British liner, the *Carmania*, before the German ship could capture or sink any enemy vessels. The fast liner *Kaiser Wilhelm der Grosse* sank the New Zealand ship, the *Kaipara*, and another freighter before herself being sunk by *HMS Highflyer* off the Spanish colony of Rio de Oro (now Western Sahara). A third German passenger ship, the *Kronprinz Wilhelm*, was in New York at the outbreak of war and put to sea to meet the *Karlsruhe* from which she obtained guns; in eight months in the South Atlantic she sank seventeen Allied ships before sailing into internment in the United States. She simply could not carry on: the engines were in poor shape and coal supplies were almost exhausted by the time *Konprinz Wilhelm* sailed into Newport News, Virginia.

Several merchantmen, more thoroughly converted to surface raiders in German dockyards, attempted to run the British blockade and make for the North Atlantic. The *Greif* was caught trying to run the blockade by the cruisers *Alcantara* and *Andes* which sent her to the bottom with the loss of ninety-seven men. Apart from the *Wolf* and the *Seeadler* (which features in later chapters), only one other made it successfully through the blockade. She was the *Moewe*, built in 1914 for the West African trade, and in two cruises she sank forty ships and mined the Pentland Firth off the north of Scotland, one mine sinking the battleship *King Edward VII*. From both cruises, the *Moewe* returned safely to Germany although she was involved in two battles with two armed merchantmen which resisted capture.

The last raider to be sent out was a captured and converted British merchantman *Yarrowdale* and, renamed *Leopard*, was another to fail to get through the blockade. Set upon by the cruisers *Archilleus* and *Dundee*, 319 men went down with the raider.

Was it all worth it? The activities of the raiders, while capturing the imagination of the public both in Germany and the British Empire, did not seriously diminish the British merchant fleet; no ship would emulate the achievement by *Emden* of disrupting movements of goods and Imperial troops. The Germans made the mistake of inadequate planning of their raiding activities. While much attention had been given over the years to the provision of staging posts around the world where German vessels could coal and provision in time of war, it seems too little time and planning was devoted to supplying a foreign fleet which could have used these *etappen*. The *Moewe*, *Wolf* and *Seeadler* were sent out as independent marauders. How much more effective they would have been if there had been a concerted plan of action is open to conjecture, but the captains of the *Seeadler* and the *Moewe* were at one stage operating in the same part of the Atlantic without realising the fact.

At a time when the *Wolf* and the *Seeadler* were converging on the Pacific and seas around Australasia, neither Australia nor New Zealand had any adequate naval defence, the number of ships available being greatly diminished by war needs elsewhere in the world. In March 1917 the Australian Naval Board, which knew that, if the Australian fleet had not been in existence, then the *Emden* and any other raider could have attacked shipping out of Australasian ports with impunity. A report on the disposition of the fleet submitted to the Admiralty in London noted that in 1917 the *Australia, Melbourne, Sydney* and *Brisbane* were all serving in European waters, that the *HMAS Psyche* (which New Zealand had had in its waters in 1914 and had now returned to the Australians), the *Fantome* and three destroyers were attached to the British China Station. *HMAS Encounter* was stationed to protect shipping off south-western Australia. Three other destroyers were stationed at, respectively, Jervis Bay, Twofold Bay and Bass Strait for patrols on the main shipping lane between Sydney and Melbourne.

The board noted that at times, due to ships either relieving with the China Station or undergoing refits, Australian waters had been left largely unprotected. It was known at this stage that some sort of raider was at work in the Indian Ocean and on 3 April 1917 the *Encounter* was ordered to New Zealand to escort a troop convoy to Fremantle, where it was augmented with Australian troopships, and on to Colombo. Australia had nothing larger than a destroyer left in its waters, and the Naval Board, clearly exasperated, cabled London for some help in safeguarding Australia's coasts and shipping. Three days later the decision was made to send Japanese ships to Australia.

A number of Japanese ships had paid calls to Australian and New Guinean ports in the early years of the war escorting a number of troop convoys and patrolling the main Indian Ocean shipping lanes, particularly those out of Fremantle. As a result of these latest Australian requests, the light cruisers the *Hirado* and the *Chikuma* were assigned to protect Australia for most of the remainder of 1917. They spent some months operating out of Sydney and Jervis Bay, and separately visited Melbourne, Hobart,

Townsville, Brisbane and, several New Zealand ports as well as patrolling northwards to the New Hebrides, New Guinea and Fiji. Three other Japanese ships made occasional sweeps down the coast of Western Australia during 1917, giving many Australians the lasting impression Japan was solely responsible for guarding the Pacific Ocean and for escorting Australian troops safely across the Indian Ocean. The official history of Australia's naval role in the Great War later argued that it was misleading to believe Allied naval defence in the Pacific was solely a Japanese concern, but without the vessels from Britain's Asian ally there would have been no meaningful defence at sea for Australia and New Zealand during much of 1917. Not that their presence was particularly reassuring, especially for the New Zealanders.

The legacy of the 'Yellow Peril' fears, which raged in both Dominions at the end of the nineteenth century, was still strong in the minds of many people. New Zealand's government firmly believed that, while the Germans posed a present and clear danger, ultimately the British Dominions would face peril from Japan. The alacrity with which the Tokyo government had occupied German islands in the mid-Pacific had not been lost on Wellington. Across the Tasman similar fears were held by the Federal government in Melbourne, and both countries were uneasy about a British under-taking to support Japan's continued occupation of the Marshall and other islands of German Micronesia. In 1918 Australian Prime Minister Billy Hughes asked New Zealand's William Massey to help him oppose the move when it came to a peace conference, but the New Zealand Prime Minister was much more concerned with advancing his own country's claim to Western Samoa when the time came.

New Zealand's own defences at sea were practically non-existent after 1915. As we have noted, the *Psyche* was returned to Australia, while the *Philomel* and the *Pyramus* operated in the Red

Sea, Persian Gulf and Mediterranean. In January 1917, when the *Wolf* was starting her raids in the Indian Ocean and moving toward Australia and New Zealand, the *Pyramus* was probably (her log was lost after the war) in the Gulf of Aden while the *Philomel* was on passage from Muscat to Bombay. Both ships were clearly at the end of their effective working lives, and the New Zealand government was more and more concerned with building (and controlling) its own naval force, crewed totally by New Zealanders.

The major lesson of the war had been that Britain, in a jam, would be too preoccupied with its own problems (in the naval theatre, the threat from German submarines to its lines of supply across the Atlantic and from the brooding menace of the German High Seas Fleet across the North Sea) to worry much about Australia and New Zealand. It was a lesson which was not learned properly until World War II and, particularly, the fall of Singapore.

*   *   *

There were two raiders named *Wolf*. The first, the former merchantman *Belgravia*, had been stranded off the small island of Neuwerk in the North Sea after an accident in its engine room. Her engines were so badly strained that she could not be allowed to continue the voyage and was towed back to port by tugs, complete with her 7,000 tons of coal and 600 mines, the latter intended for British shipping in the Indian Ocean.

The second *Wolf* was the converted Hansa Line ship *Wachtfels* of 5,925 tons. This vessel was armed with seven 15-millimetre guns, four 560-millimetre torpedo tubes, 465 mines and a Friedrichshafen E33 seaplane. Her commander, Karl August Nerger, had previously commanded a light cruiser. He was the opposite of the *Emden*'s commander. He was not noted for being cool or phlegmatic; several prisoners aboard *Wolf* later recalled how Nerger had flown into passionate anger whenever something went wrong, shouting at the erring crew members, and then just as quickly reverting to calm.

His new ship had been built in 1913 and was converted to an auxiliary raider in 1916, being commissioned by the German navy on 16 May that year. Coal-fired (and modified to have very large coal bunkers) she had a maximum speed of ten knots and a range of 42,000 nautical miles at nine knots which gave her a cruising endurance of 194 days. When compared to the *Cormoran* or the *Prinz Eitel Friedrich*, which had cruising endurances of forty and thirty days respectively, it is possible to understand why the *Wolf* was so much more effective. It also supports criticism of the German naval planners: one ship specifically converted for raider activities with properly prepared coal bunkers showed up the inadequacies of those other vessels hurriedly turned into marauders at the outbreak of war and left to their own devices. It was a lesson the Germans had learned by World War II when their raiders had huge oil capacity; ships such as the *Atlantis* had a cruising range of 60,000 nautical miles (250 days) and the *Kormoran* 84,500 nautical miles at ten knots (352 days).

Apart from its aeroplane, which was loaded aboard in parts to be assembled when needed, the *Wolf's* most useful innovation was the mounting of the torpedo-tubes on swivel-mounts, thus avoiding the need for the ship to be swung and pointed at the target. Particular attention was given to the locations of the guns and torpedo tubes as they had to be concealed behind flats which were lowered as the ship cleared for action.

The *Wolf's* first venture to sea had to be aborted when fire broke out in the coal bunker; not an unusual event in the days of steamers. The fire was uncomfortably close to the huge stores of ammunition. The crew successfully battled the flames knowing what would happen if the fire spread.

Three weeks were lost while, back in port, the crew emptied the bunkers of the now useless coal, cleaned the ship, and re-bunkered. On 30 November she was ready once again. She sailed out of Kiel with the name *Jupiter* on her stern; this name was painted out once at sea. She looked every bit the slow collier, with a black hull, white superstructure, and one tall smokestack. Her weapons were cunningly hidden from view and there was nothing to suggest that *Wolf* was anything other than a harmless steamer. It was not until 10 December that the German raider was safely in the Atlantic.

In order to avoid the British cruiser blockade designed to prevent German ships getting out or supplies getting in, Nerger steered his vessel northwards along the Norwegian coast, turning north-west near Bergen. His plan was to sail north as far as he dare in the winter to try and evade the British. The bad weather he hoped for eventuated, making it difficult — if not impossible — for British ships to sight the *Wolf*. Storm after storm of wind and snow pounded the ship as it beat westward through the blizzards. The ship bucketed and rolled, freezing water sweeping across the deck, the guns iced up. Slowly the ship edged its way to the north of Iceland, then turned southwards through the Denmark Strait and into the Atlantic.

Nerger set a course which was designed to avoid other shipping, so that *Wolf* sailed a route down the middle of the Atlantic. As the days grew warmer the men were able to relax on deck, drinking beer and reading. They sighted a few ships, but Nerger's orders were to avoid action in the Atlantic. So the harmless-looking ship pottered on. The crew-members were not privy to

Nerger's orders to concentrate efforts in the Indian Ocean and so were disappointed that they had made no attacks.

As far as the British were concerned, the raiding by the *Moewe* had put them on alert for further trouble. In June 1916 Admirals Rosslyn Wemyss (commander of the East Indies Station) and Heathcote Grant had met at Colombo to discuss the problem. Their plan was to divert merchant and passenger ships from the normal sea routes in the Indian Ocean and to assign naval ships to patrol areas where a concentration of shipping could not be avoided. The ships would be given assigned routes, with no two consecutive vessels using the same route between any two ports. The most critical area was between Aden and Colombo. The Red Sea and Suez could be patrolled thoroughly, but the Arabian Sea was a vast proposition even for the Royal Navy. Hundreds of ships plied these waters, not just from India, but also from British Empire territories in east Asia, from the China coast and from Australia and New Zealand. In the Bay of Bengal similar precautions were planned for the sea lanes between Colombo, Calcutta and Rangoon. Dispersion was not possible given the number of narrow waterways on approaches to harbours, so that naval protection was particularly crucial near Calcutta and Colombo, at the Andaman Islands, and particularly in the Malacca Straits, 665 kilometres long, through which all the shipping from Singapore was channelled.

The British had only a limited number of cruisers for these patrols, so that the Straits of Malacca — like the waters around Australia and New Zealand — were left to the Japanese Navy to guard. In January 1917, as Nerger rounded the Cape of Good Hope, the Allies had fifty-five ships stationed in the Indian Ocean. Several small vessels were at South African ports or at ports in what had been German East Africa; the 12,000 ton armoured cruiser (and Wemyss's flagship) *Euryalus* was refitting at Bombay. A good number of smaller ships could be found in the seas between Aden and Colombo. Of the Australian destroyers, the *Huon* was at Jesselton in British North Borneo (now Kota Kinabalu in Sabah) and the *Torrens* and the *Swan* were patrolling off Singapore. In February the cruiser *Newcastle* was ordered to Colombo, the Japanese cruisers *Niitaka* and *Tsushima* were sent to the Cape of Good Hope while three French ships, the *Pothuau*, the *D'Entrecasteaux* and the *D' Estrees* were placed under British command by the French admiral at Djibouti. The British not only feared the ability of a well-armed raider to sink their ships, but were also worried the Germans would attempt to free and arm any of the many German freighters interned in the neutral ports of the Dutch East Indies. In fact the *Wolf* was carrying three guns which had been designated to be handed over to other auxiliaries if that became possible.

On 16 January 1917 Nerger and his crew sighted the coast of South Africa near the Cape of Good Hope while to sea the look-outs spotted several plumes of smoke later found to be six troop transports under the protection of the British cruiser *Cornwall*. Nerger was not alarmed as night was falling and he knew his ship was unlikely to arouse suspicion before it took its first victim.

His plan was to lay mines, an operation which required great skill and judgement. It was necessary to take into account the tides, in which direction ships would be travelling, and their size. The mines had to be laid diagonally across the chosen sea lane, and reasonably far apart to prevent them hitting one another and exploding (and taking the minelayer with them). It was a job best suited to darkness when the ship's unusual manoeuvres would not arouse suspicion. The mines were laid about five metres below the surface so only large vessels would strike them; the value of sinking a small ship was outweighed by the fact that the field would be swept by the British once it was discovered. Together the mine and anchor weighed about five hundred kilograms with about 160 kilograms of high explosive in each mine. The *Wolf's* mines were stored behind doors in the stern with extending rails to allow the mines to drop well clear of the ship. It took several hours to lay about twenty-five mines. The doors, naturally, were designed so that they were not noticeable to the casual observer.

Should the *Wolf* be surprised while laying mines, or when it was ready to pounce on an Allied ship, the guns could be ready for action within minutes. The stern gun was disguised as a derrick, the tarpaulin coming off with the pull of a dummy block, and all the ventilators on the deck were collapsible to allow the gun a free swing. Other guns were hidden behind the collapsible, hinged sides on the afterdeck, the forward deck and the raised monsoon deck at the bow.

That night fifty mines were laid off Cape Town. They were placed off Saldanha Bay say they would lie in the course of vessels heading northwards from the Cape of Good Hope. The day after, another fifty mines were laid off Cape Agulhas, to the east of Cape Town.

The mines were not to claim their first victim until 25 January. Meanwhile, on 18 January the British learned that the *Moewe* was operating off the River Plate and the ports of Montevideo and Buenos Aires. Unaware that the *Wolf* was also lurking, the British relaxed their guard in the Indian Ocean. On 24 January, Admiral Grant ordered the withdrawal of the patrols outside Colombo and Penang. By that time Nerger was about to lay seventy-five mines south of Bombay and a further 100 near Colombo.

On 25 January the British freighters, the *Matheran* and the *Portugal*, struck the mines at Saldanha Bay, the former sinking while the *Portugal* survived to be towed to port. For several days the British suspected torpedoes from a submarine. For a day all sailings for South Africa were stopped. On 1 February it was confirmed that the cause of the explosions was a minefield, and that only a surface raider could be responsible. Even with fifty-five warships at their disposal, the Allies had a daunting task in finding the Germans.

The sinking of the 7,000 ton passenger ship *Worcestershire* with the loss of twelve lives at the minefield near Colombo on 10 February put the British on full alert. For Nerger, it was time to keep moving, trying to stay one step ahead of what would now be a pursuit. The first victim provided an ironic twist. Off the northern end of the Maldive Islands — which had been so profitably raided by the *Emden* — Nerger spied a ship which looked unnervingly like his own. After firing a shot across the bow of the vessel flying the British ensign, a boarding party was dispatched. When the ship's papers were examined, it was discovered that she was the *Wolf's* (or, more correctly, the *Wachtfels'*) sister ship, the former *Gutenfels*, the ex-Hansa Line ship having been captured by the British at the outbreak of war and renamed the *Turritella*. Nerger was unwilling to sink what was really a German ship, so he hit upon the idea of turning her into an auxiliary. She was given the name of *Ilitis*. Her career in the Imperial German Navy was to last all of three weeks. One of the *Wolf's* officers, Kapitanleutnant Iwan Brandes was given command and equipped with one of the small guns put aboard the *Wolf* at Kiel for just this eventuality. More importantly, the new raider also took aboard mines; Nerger had decided to despatch her to lay them at the approaches to the British base of Aden.

That night *Ilitis* sailed off into the gathering dusk, leaving her former officers as the *Wolf's* first prisoners; the Chinese crew remained on board *Ilitis*. The *Turritella's* captain, J. G. Meadows, was a New Zealander, and he would be joined by several fellow countrymen before many weeks were out.

On 1 March as the *Ilitis* steamed away and Nerger worked around the Maldives he came upon his second victim, the 4,235 ton British freighter *Jumna* bound for Calcutta. She had coal which Nerger unloaded, after which he sank her with an explosive charge. Brandes, aboard *Ilitis* off Aden, was not so lucky. Just as he completed laying his mines, he was spotted from the Royal Navy sloop *Odin* which had been sent to sea to observe whether the Aden township had been effectively blacked out. The *Odin's* captain, Lieutenant Commander E.M. Palmer, was aware that there was another ship nearby, without lights but clearly visible on a perfectly fine. moonlit night. A neutral ship would have been showing her lights. After gaining an unsatisfactory answer to his signal seeking identification and destination, Palmer ordered the other vessel to stop. The mystery ship answered: 'Why did you not stop me when I passed Aden? Meadows, master.' Palmer's suspicions were now thoroughly aroused, and he pursued the strange ship, using his searchlight to keep on her tail after the moon set. Soon after sun-up, the sloop's commander saw boats being lowered and, as these pulled away from the *Ilitis*, two huge explosions were heard, upon which the vessel settled slowly. The Chinese crew members had no hesitation in telling the British what they had seen and heard. The British now had a full description of the *Wolf*, including the fact that she had a seaplane.

Nerger knew better than to hang about. The British would soon be swarming all over the Indian Ocean looking for him. The *Wolf* headed for Australia; she passed south of the Great Australian Bight, sailing through the southern section of the Tasman Sea and around New Zealand until she reached the Kermadec Islands.

Throughout that long journey, only two ships fell into Nerger's hands. On 11 March in mid-Indian Ocean, smoke was sighted, the aircraft (named *Wölfchen*) was launched and reported a freighter. She had found the 3,580-ton *Wordsworth*, bound for London with a cargo of rice. The passengers and some coal were taken aboard, then the merchantman was sunk. Moving southwards to the latitude of Fremantle, the *Wolf* intercepted a three-masted barque *Dee* (1,192 tons) in ballast from Mauritius. She too was sunk after the crew had been disembarked.

Nerger and his three hundred men had been at sea now for four months, and they did not have all that much to show for it. None of the ships they had sunk had been of vital strategic value (except, perhaps, the *Wordsworth* and her valuable cargo of food destined for Britain). South of Australia and New Zealand the sea lanes were deserted. Nerger spent two totally barren and unprofitable months in those uninviting seas in what seems to have been a belief that he would find grain ships and colliers London-bound from Australian ports. The seas in that region are as hostile as any the Germans had endured while eluding the British blockade in the North Sea (it rains for all but thirty or forty days of the year, the winds howl relentlessly, and huge waves batter and buffet any ship which ventures there). Nerger, therefore, had to find somewhere to rest up, to allow his crew to recover and, more importantly, to find more profitable raiding. He settled on the Kermadec Islands north of New Zealand.

8

At Large in the Tasman Sea

THE KERMADEC ISLANDS LIE at thirty degrees of latitude north-east of New Zealand. In 1886 British sovereignty was proclaimed over them and they were formally annexed to New Zealand the following year. The largest island — Raoul, or Sunday Island as it was known in 1917 — covers nearly 3,000 hectares. The islands had been settled in 1837 by two families who grew crops to supply food to the many whaling vessels which called at the island. All the settlers left in 1872 after volcanic disturbances. In 1878 Thomas Bell had arrived with his wife and five young children to re-establish the plantation. After annexation by New Zealand the land was subdivided and a few more settlers arrived. The island was once again evacuated on the outbreak of war in 1914. Nerger was well aware the island was uninhabited but that there were abandoned plantations which would provide food for his men. There was plenty of fruit on the trees when they arrived.

Nerger took the opportunity to carry out necessary maintenance on his ship. From 22 May until 2 June the engineers toiled at overhauling the boilers after the strains of several months at sea.

The raider's captain had to rely on the eyes of his two aviators who took the seaplane aloft daily to watch for an enemy vessel.

On 2 June they saw one. She was the Union Steam Ship Company freighter *Wairuna*, sailing from Auckland to San Francisco with a valuable general cargo: forty sheep (which would provide fresh meat), 350 tons of fresh water and 1,100 tons of coal. She was quite a prize after the previous thankless months. The *Wolf* could not raise steam in time to pursue the New Zealand ship, so *Wolfchen* flew low over the *Wairuna*, dropping a message warning the captain not to use his wireless or the aircraft would bomb his vessel. Captain Harold Saunders decided to obey as he no doubt realised that a heavily armed raider would eventually catch up.

Many of the subsequent events aboard the *Wolf* were recollected twenty years after the event by the wireless operator aboard the *Wairuna*, Roy Alexander, whose account of the voyage remains the most detailed source. He and his fellow crew members now found themselves locked up aboard the German raider with the crews of the *Wordsworth*, the *Dee* and other captured ships. Breakfast that first morning of captivity consisted of coffee and black bread and, as it was a Sunday, the crew of the *Wolf* had the afternoon off listening to the band. On the Monday work began on stripping the *Wairuna*. It was to take two weeks — largely due to bouts of bad weather — during which time the captives were allowed to fish from the deck. The subsequent disappearance of two prisoners from the ship — they had been taken captive from the *Turritella* —ended this lax control. The two men had slipped over the side intending to swim to Sunday Island, conceal themselves in the dense bush, and live off the land until they could be rescued. They were never heard of again; it was assumed that they had been caught by the sharks which were common in the waters around the Kermadec group.

By 17 June everything usable had been taken aboard the *Wolf*. The *Wairuna* was towed to sea to be sent to the bottom but this proved to be a great deal harder than the Germans had bargained for; two bombs placed on her keel failed to do the job, and it was only after thirty-six shells fired from the *Wolf's* guns that the *Wairuna* rolled slowly on to her port side and began to sink.

Because the *Wairuna* had not sent out a wireless distress signal when she had had the chance, the *Wolf* could continue to raid in the South Pacific with impunity. Nerger was to find himself largely in the debt of Australian wireless operators over the next few months. Their uncoded messages would later bring him the passenger liner *Matunga* but as *Wolf* headed away from the Kermadec he now learned from those radio signals that the 578-ton sailing schooner *Winslow* had left Sydney for Apia. The *Winslow* with a crew of fifteen, which now became the latest victim, was carrying supplies of great use to Nerger, including firebricks for the furnaces, coal for the bunkers and benzine for the seaplane. Nerger put back to Sunday Island to strip this latest prize and, on 22 June, the schooner was towed out to sea. Again two bombs were placed on her bottom and, although her stern was ripped apart by the explosions, the four-master would not sink. Again the German gunners had to send shells screaming into their victim — thirty-nine of them — but even these could not finish the job. Fire was then started on what remained of the wooden vessel, but that did not work either. Large pieces of the *Winslow* were thus washed ashore on Sunday Island as evidence of the *Wolf's* work.

The raider now headed for the coast of New Zealand to lay mines. Things were starting to look up for Nerger and his men. The ship had been at sea for six months but several mechanical problems had been successfully repaired; the capture of coal had put off, at least for the time being, the necessity for the crew to bring up coal from the *Wolf's* lower hold and transfer it to the bunkers, a backbreaking job. There had been excursions ashore at Sunday Island, plenty of fresh fruit, meat and water. There was still the continuing problem of weed growth on the hull which was slowing the *Wolf* down. (Later, however, the strain would start tell on Nerger's crew and, after months at sea, bad food would result in scurvy.)

During the night of 25 June, the prisoners heard the stern doors being opened, and the rails run out for mine laying. Twenty-five mines were dropped into the sea between Cape Maria van Diemen at the northern tip of New Zealand and Three Kings Islands, right in the middle of the sea lanes used by ships plying between Auckland and Australian ports.

New Zealand's mountainous terrain dictated that coastal shipping was still a vital form of transport in 1917. The railway between Wellington and Auckland had been completed only in 1908; the trunk line running from the top of the South Island at Picton to Christchurch would not be completed until 1945. Many coastal settlements had a port but no railway.

After laying her first batch of mines the *Wolf* steamed down along the west coast of New Zealand. Nerger's plan was to stay in the Tasman and later move across to the Australian coast. On 27 and 28 June *Wolf* laid a further thirty-five mines at Cape Farewell, a point which had to be passed by any ship approaching Cook Strait from the Tasman Sea. The narrow strait which separates the two main islands of New Zealand was always busy with shipping. For ships approaching New Zealand en route from Australia, the beam from the lighthouse at Cape Farewell was the first sign of landfall. Apart from the intercolonial vessels sailing between Wellington and the Australian ports, colliers turned at the cape after coming up the coast from Westport and Greymouth. Coastal ships heading for the ports of Nelson and Motueka (on the northern coast of the South Island) would also pass close to where the mines were laid.

Now Nerger turned out into the Tasman Sea, heading for Australia where he would lay mines off the coast near the Victoria-New South Wales border, right in the middle of the main shipping lane between Sydney and Melbourne. The most extraordinary aspect of the *Wolf's* crossing the Tasman Sea this time was that she had sailed close to the main shipping routes, being sighted by several ships but suspected by none. Nerger, meanwhile, was too intent on laying his mines to risk an attack on any of the ships he saw in these busy waters. The transfer of coal or other material was an operation which, as they knew from experience, would involve considerable time. Supplies were needed: food, particularly for the prisoners, was starting to run short. Their diet by this stage consisted of black bread and coffee, supplemented with preserved meat and rice or potatoes once a day.

Some accounts have it that the cruiser *Encounter* passed the *Wolf* while the Germans were in the middle of their mine-laying activities; but the official record states that the Australian ship was in Port Philip at the time so it is more likely that the idea was born of taut nerves among the raider's crew who, like their fellows aboard the *Emden*, were overworked and tense after months of potential danger on the high seas. One night a German guard completely lost control and fired into a row of hammocks in the prisoners' quarters; fortunately no one was hit.

The first victim of these mines off Australia came just three days after they were laid. The *Cumberland*, a 9,660-ton steamer belonging to the Federal Steam Navigation Company, had left Sydney on 5 July 1917 bound for England via South Africa with mails and what was reported at the time as a cargo of meat; however, when in 1951 salvage crews worked on the ship they found 1,825 tons of copper and lead ingots. The next day *Cumberland* reported by wireless that she was sinking sixteen kilometres off Gabo Island. Her captain, A.G. McGibbon, turned the two-year old ship toward the shore in order to beach her. The first vessel to reach her was the Japanese warship *Chikuma*, which, after anchoring near the stricken freighter, sent a diver below. He reported that there was a large hole measuring over three by six metres which opened outwards. 'This fully illustrates that her explosion occurred from inside and not from outside', stated Admiral Yamaji aboard the *Chikuma*, even though McGibbon had wirelessed at the time that he had struck a mine. The admiral added that his diver's report suggested that it was not a mine which was responsible for the explosion and sinking of the British ship.

The Federal Steam Navigation Co vessel Cumberland *lying wrecked at Gabo Island on 7 July 1917.* [Australian War Memorial A710]

Australian newspapers ran the story of this apparently heinous deed on their own doorstep. The *Sydney Morning Herald*, on 9 July, reported a Navy Office announcement that the ship had been damaged by 'internal explosions in one of the holds'. The crew members themselves believed that the explosion had been internal; just after it occurred they had looked over the sides and saw carcasses of meat pouring from the hull as if a force had been behind them. They dismissed the suggestion by the *Daily Telegraph* that the *Cumberland* had struck a mine. 'All the jagged ends of the plates', they explained, 'project outward'. Suspicion devolved upon the radical workers movement, the Industrial Workers of the World, who were to be also later blamed for planting a bomb aboard the *Port Kembla* (which was soon to be sunk off New Zealand). By the end of August Prime Minister Billy Hughes was offering £2,000 by way of reward 'for information leading to the conviction of the criminal or criminals implicated in the wreck of the steamer the *Cumberland*, and to the full disclosure of the methods employed in the perpetration of the crime'. The New South Wales Government and the British Board of Trade each added a further £1,000.

A detailed report issued by the investigation branch of the Commonwealth Attorney-General's Department stated the Japanese diver had been misled by the haste with which his observations had necessarily been made and that, in fact, all the evidence obtained by the Australian investigators showed that placing a bomb at the point within the vessel where the explosion occurred was practically impossible. The only conclusion they could draw was that the freighter had hit a mine.

It was not an opinion that the Australian Naval Board wanted to endorse. An internal explosion was still the favoured theory in that quarter. To settle the matter, trawlers with minesweeping gear were sent to the area. By early January 1918 they had found twelve mines. Further mines continued to be discovered over the next two years, while the last one found was washed up on the beach at Noosa Heads in Queensland in February 1921.

Meanwhile, the mines laid near the entrance to New Zealand's Cook Strait claimed their first victim in September 1917. The British vessel *Port Kembla* struck a mine just fifteen nautical miles north of Cape Farewell. While the mails and cargo were lost, the crew and passengers all got safely into the boats and were blessed by a calm sea. No lives were lost and all those aboard were picked by the steamer *Regulus* which was on its regular Nelson–Westport run.

Then at 5.05 am on 25 June 1918 the 3,082-ton Huddart Parker liner *Wimmera* struck one of the mines off Cape Maria van Diemen on a voyage from Auckland to Sydney with seventy-six passengers and seventy-five crew. The most extraordinary aspect was that New Zealand authorities had found eleven of the mines laid there by *Wolf* prior to the *Wimmera* sailing. The master, Captain Kell, could not have been unaware of them. One theory is that he had decided to pass through the mined area out of sheer obstinacy. The explosion was at the stern where most of the passenger accommodation was located. Several passengers were killed outright. The lights failed immediately, as did the power supply to the wireless so that no distress signal was sent. Fortunately, most of the passengers who survived the explosion were able to find their way through the dark passageways — it was midwinter and so still dark outside — and on to the decks and the life boats. The liner went down within half an hour, water pouring in through gaping holes in the ship's hull. The boats reached shore safely the next day. Kell was last seen on the bridge, apparently making no effort to save himself. He was one of twenty-seven people to lose their lives in the sinking. A court of inquiry found he had ignored confidential Admiralty advice.

SS Wimmera, *the Huddart Parker liner sunk by mines laid by* Wolf. [Mitchell Library]

Both the *Cumberland* and the *Wimmera* were sunk in waters they had been warned to avoid, the former having been told by shipping authorities in Sydney to keep outside the 100 fathom line, as mines were likely to have been laid in shallower waters.

Even though the New Zealand authorities (whom Roy Alexander described as having 'an incapacity so hopeless that it remains almost incredible') had been alerted to the finding of the mines, they did little to develop any sort of minesweeping fleet. Eventually, they acted, in January 1918 chartering three fishing vessels to sweep for mines in New Zealand waters. These found forty-seven of the sixty mines laid by the Germans. (It is believed that, apart from the incidents covered in this book, the following ships were also lost to mines laid by the *Wolf* in other regions it traversed: the British ships the *Cilicia* and the *City of Athens*, the Spanish vessel *Ciudad de Fizaguiree* off Cape Town, the British

Perseus off Colombo, the British *Mongolia*, *Okhla* and *Croxteth Hall* and the Japanese *Unkai Maru*, all off Bombay.)

By the time that it was realised in Australia and New Zealand that the mines had probably been laid by a German raider, the *Wolf* was long gone. In early July 1917 Nerger had ordered a course northwards in order to lurk along the Sydney to Suva shipping lane. The prisoners were allowed on deck for an hour a day (they were usually allowed up when a ship was captured, Nerger believing it relieved the dreadful boredom). Roy Alexander, standing in the cold air, half-starved and shivering, looked out over the dark sea and recalled all those other voyages across the Tasman; he remembered the passengers on the *Manuka* complaining there was no orchestra or those aboard the *Mokoia* grumbling the ship could make only thirteen knots. Now at least the prison ship was heading northwards, into warmer climes and calmer seas, and the men began to wash again as conditions became more comfortable.

They would soon be joined by a woman and her child. They were the captain's family on the American barque *Beluga* (500 tons), an ex-whaler now laden with benzine and heading for Sydney. While the master's wife and child were being shown to a cabin aboard the German ship, the *Wolf's* guns opened up on the latest victim. Soon it was ablaze, the benzine producing flames that licked the masts and covered the surrounding sea as the burning fuel leaked from the splintered hull, the Germans having already taken all they needed for their aeroplane. Nine days later they captured the American schooner the *Encore* (664 tons) bound for Sydney with a cargo of timber. She too was quickly despatched.

Nerger was happy to sink any Allied ship that came his way but what he now wanted was a collier. None was to be seen. The *Wolf* hung about the Suva route waiting, while down below the crews from the two sailing ships tried to find some room for themselves. As the ship lumbered along under the watery winter sun, the prisoners would sit out on the deck, playing cards and talking. The only interruptions to this routine were the basic and monotonously same meals, and the tropical downpours during which the men would strip off and wash. Fights were common, and the German crew aboard the *Wolf* was not of the chivalrous type that had crewed the *Emden*. There was no possibility that the prisoners would be giving the Germans three cheers after this voyage was over. There was to be a serious incident later while the *Wolf* was anchored in the Dutch East Indies. In the meantime the level of argument and resentment mounted, especially as the mixture of men was increased with each ship that was captured. The fact that the prisoners had been locked up for twenty-eight days in the hold after the escape of two of their number in the Kermadec Islands, that they were allowed only a brief exercise period and were fed very badly added terribly to the strain. There was no doubt that the quick-tempered Nerger was not the ideal man to relieve the daily growing tension on his ship.

Nerger sailed toward Fiji and then cut back past the New Hebrides and the Solomon Islands. Still no sign of a collier. Then, on 28 July, he intercepted a wireless message from Sydney. It read: 'Burns Philp Rabaul. Donaldson left Sydney on 27th via Newcastle Brisbane, 340 tons general cargo, 500 tons Westport coal Rabaul, 236 tons general cargo Madang. Burns.' According to the routines of contact between Papua New Guinea and Australia, there being no cable connection, wireless messages contained no ships' names, but they were identified by the names of their masters. In 1917 the rather lax regulations on wireless traffic between ships and Australian stations had been strengthened. Private messages were forbidden and those between ship and agents and owners were to be kept to a minimum. Wheat carriers and other merchant ships were told to signal only in an emergency or to signal a port twenty-four hours in advance to alert the port to its arrival time. It was considered, therefore, reasonable for the Burns Philp company to send the message that it did, being between owner and agent. At that stage, however, Nerger did not know the identity of the ship; after all, that was the point of using the master's name in messages. Any raider could be expected to carry information of the names of ships, and perhaps details such as size and the number of funnels. But there was no way they could keep track of who was master of which ship. Even so, the regulations as they were, even after being 'tightened', seem remarkably casual.

The ship's identity was revealed to Nerger the next day when Captain Alex Donaldson despatched a wireless signal from the *Matunga*: '7.43 pm. VHV to VIB. Burns Philp Brisbane. Cape Moreton noon Monday. Donaldson.' The ship's call sign gave the game away completely; now the Germans knew which ship was carrying the Westport coal they so desperately needed.

Donaldson was quite unconcerned as the 1,618-ton steel passenger steamer worked its passage toward Rabaul. When he had reported to the naval authorities in Sydney on 27 July to get his instructions, he was told the sinking of the *Cumberland* earlier that month had been caused not by a mine but an internal explosion. 'And so', Donaldson wrote later, 'I departed from Sydney quite cheerfully'. His passengers included Colonel Cecil Strangman, principle medical officer for New Britain, several military men and three civilians who had special permission to travel owing to their interests in the former German Solomon Islands. It was a pleasant and peaceful run up the Australian coast and on 5 August Donaldson sent out another wireless message, overheard aboard the *Wolf* as well as in Rabaul: 'Burns Philp Rabaul. Arriving Tuesday 2 am. Arrange Burrows coal direct. Donaldson.' The Burrows referred to in the message was the commander of the *HMAS Una* (formerly the German *Komet* captured in the first weeks of the war); Donaldson planned to tie up at the wharf at Rabaul and discharge his cargo while at the same time *Una* would come alongside on his seaward side to take off the coal. This part of the message confused Nerger. The only Burrows that made any sense to him was an American destroyer by that name. It was therefore necessary for him to intercept the *Matunga* as far from Rabaul as possible if there was a warship waiting in that port. As Rabaul had received a specific estimated time of arrival from Donaldson, the failure of his ship to arrive on time would mean that the alarm would be raised shortly after. It was also necessary to take the *Matunga* before she could use her wireless. The *Wolf* ploughed through the seas heading for her quarry.

The Matunga, *a Burns Philp vessel which radioed her position to Rabaul, so telling the Germans exactly where she was. This photograph was taken in New Guinea in 1914, three years before her end.* [Australian War Memorial J3109]

On the night of 5 August Nerger found what he was after. There was the *Matunga* all lit up as if it were still peacetime. The *Wolf* shadowed the unsuspecting freighter through the night, the German ship totally blacked out so that her intended victim could not see her.

The next morning as Captain Donaldson crossed the bridge on the way to his bath his chief officer reported that the *Morinda*, an island steamer, was passing to the west. She was due to return to Sydney with mails and copra (no use to Nerger). Donaldson, however, knew that this could not be because the *Morinda* was not due to leave Rabaul until later that day.

His own view, given that the ship was on the same heading as his own, was that she was probably Japanese. He had seen a similar looking Japanese auxiliary raider at Rabaul on one of his previous voyages. Thus satisfied, he went off to have his bath. As the *Wolf* drew closer, it became clear that she was German built, but as many such ships had been interned at the start of the war and were now operated by Australian crews, he still felt no sense of alarm.

Signal flags were hoisted by the *Wolf*: 'Telegraph communication stopped', followed by 'Stop instantly'. The *Matunga's* best speed was seven and a half knots — she could not outrun the raider. A live shot across the bows and the sight of the *Wolfchen* overhead removed any lingering doubts in Donaldson's mind. He immediately ordered the boats swung out, assuming that the raider would sink his ship and expect the crew and passengers to make land in the boats.

In charge of the boarding party was Leutnant Rose who, on stepping on deck, saluted Donaldson and said in English 'Good morning, Captain Donaldson. You are late, we expected you two days ago.' He then asked where the Westport coal was stored. Donaldson was perplexed by the fact that the German not only knew his name but also the nature of his cargo, until he was told about the message to Rabaul from the Sydney owners. There followed the usual procedure: the examination of the ship's papers (the code books had been quickly thrown into the furnaces when the *Matunga* had been ordered to stop), the log and the cargo lists. All the passengers were transferred to the *Wolf*.

By the evening of 7 August, a slowly rising feeling of alarm was evident back in Australia. Where was *Matunga*? After all, only two days ago she had radioed her estimated time of arrival. It was a mystery which would baffle the Australians for months; they had no idea that she had been taken by the *Wolf* to a remote bay in the Dutch East Indies and stripped. On 27 February 1918, after the *Wolf* was safely home, the Sydney *Sun* was still reporting that the fate of the *Matunga* was unknown, although one map published at that time showed with certainty that the *Matunga* had been sunk at about the point where she was captured. Even after the news was received that the *Wolf* was safely back in Germany the Navy Office in Melbourne said it had no knowledge where the crew and passengers might be. Under the headline 'Well-Informed *Wolf*', the *Sun* newspaper speculated that the raider must have had knowledge

which could only have come from Australia regarding the valuable cargo carried by the vessel. In addition to carrying 1,000 tons of coal she had extensive food supplies for the Australian troops now occupying German New Guinea. During the period the *Matunga* was in those waters the *Morinda* was also there. The *Morinda* was not even challenged. It is a fact that the *Morinda* carried hardly any cargo at all. Those on the raider must have known this, and the question arises, 'Who told them'? The Federal Government has stated that the cost of interning all enemy aliens would be prohibitive. The sum represented by the loss of the *Matunga* and its cargo alone would keep them for months.

The rather shaky logic employed by the *Sun's* journalist indicated the Australian authorities had still not owned up to the real reason why the *Wolf* had known which ship to pick, and where she could be found. Three of the four ships sunk by the *Wolf* (by mines or capture) off the coasts of Australia and New Zealand owed their fate, at least in part, to mistakes by their masters which had been compounded by the bungling of naval authorities in both countries. The evidence suggests that, with the *Emden* affair well and truly over, the governments of Australian and New Zealand had given little thought to the possibility of any danger in the Tasman Sea from German raiders even though, as examined in the previous chapter, it had been known since the previous April there had been a raider operating in the Indian Ocean. Had Nerger been a little better informed, and not wasted so much time in the ocean south of the two countries, he might well have caused a great deal more damage.

The first inkling that *Matunga* was missing came in a wireless message on 8 August from the Administrator at Rabaul. He reported to Sydney that the ship was thirty hours overdue. Meanwhile, the *Morinda* was searching around Woodlark Island (east of New Guinea's mainland) while other ships had been sent out from Rabaul to search waters around New Britain. The *Una* was also despatched to search south of New Britain. Five days later the decision was taken to advise next-of-kin that there was concern for the safety of the ship. No wreckage had been found anywhere, but the official history notes the authorities were aware of the radio signals which had been sent and that these may have alerted an enemy raider; and while noting that 'fantastic explanations' — including one that that ship was not seaworthy and had been overwhelmed after a huge submarine earthquake — were rife amongst the public, there was no rush to explain the growing suspicions in officialdom. There was also a fear the *Matunga* had been captured and was now herself an enemy raider. By September the rumours had it that the missing crew had been landed in Java, and Brisbane shuddered at the suggestion that the disappearance had been the work of spies and German sympathisers headquartered in that city. The Japanese Admiral Yamaji was of the opinion that the *Matunga* had been lost to an internal explosion, and declined to allow his warship, the *Hirado*, to join the search. The Australians combed the Solomon Sea for any sign of the missing freighter. The cruiser *Encounter*, the *Una*, the steamers *Madang, Siar, Meklong* and the mission schooner *Raphael* had covered most of that sea and the waters around the smaller islands.

By January 1918 the Australian authorities finally knew the truth, but the Admiralty instructed it be kept secret, which it was until the Germans themselves announced the safe return of the raider with her captives and booty. A bottle had been found in the sea off Sulawesi in the Celebes in Dutch East Indies and had been forwarded to the Commander of the China station by the British legation in Batavia. The message revealed that the raider had passed the Celebes on 29 August intending to mine Singapore, having already mined the North Cape of New Zealand, Cook Strait and Gabo Island off Cape Howe on the Australian coast in addition to the areas already discussed. The note listed the ships from which crews held aboard the raider had been taken. It also stated that the ship had more than a hundred mines left; one of the engineers from the *Wairuna* had been carefully counting the mines dropped, and noting their whereabouts.

No one had been anxious about the late arrival of the *Dee* or the *Winslow*; both were sailing ships and therefore at the mercy of wind and weather. The former was in ballast, so that no shipping house would have been waiting impatiently for cargo, while the latter — although anxiously awaited at Apia — was not exactly uppermost in the minds of the naval authorities in Australia.

The *Wairuna* and the *Matunga* were a different matter altogether. The *Wairuna* was owned by the Dunedin-based Union Steam Ship Company which had been controlled by the Peninsula and Orient company since 1913, but was still considered a major New Zealand flag carrier, most of its ships being registered in that country. The *Matunga* belonged to Burns Philp, a company with substantial interests (including plantations and retailing as well as shipping) in the Pacific islands and which dominated the Australian trade in that region. Both ships carried substantial and valuable cargo while *Matunga* had several important officials on its passenger list.

However, the conclusions that Australians were reaching regarding the presence of a raider resulted from incidents in which the *Wolf* played no part: a burning derelict near Christmas Island, and a report that a raider had been sighted near the Panama Canal. In September several naval ships had been sent to New Guinea waters to look for the raider, but Nerger was long gone. The *Brisbane* had been sent to the Solomon Islands and the *Encounter* and the *Hirado* in the wrong direction to Fiji.

Nerger had decided there was no time to strip the *Matunga* where he had caught her, and so had taken her well clear of New Ireland, then across the northern waters of New Guinea, where the Germans sincerely hoped no British, French or Japanese warship would have reason to be. The *Wolf* now had so many prisoners there was barely enough room for everyone, even when they were allowed on deck. Below it was worse, with men crowded together in the stinking heat of the tropics — the ship was sailing along close to the Equator. They were forced to sleep in hammocks slung in two tiers. On the second day, the two ships hove to while the boiler tubes were cleaned on the *Matunga* to enable her to keep up with the *Wolf*. In the hold the men began to reorganise their quarters.

The idea was that officers should be separated from ratings — there had already been a quarrel over an armchair used by one of the masters — and empty packing cases were reshaped to make partitions, dividing the area into one part for the captains, chief engineers and chief officers, another for the junior officers, and a third for the crews. The one great disadvantage was that the cases, which were used as lockers as well as partitions, became the home and breeding ground for lice and other vermin. Had the *Wolf* been involved in action with an enemy ship, any resulting fire might have easily spread to the prisoners' quarters, in which case the makeshift partitions would have been a serious fire hazard. The only people not subjected to these wretched conditions, apart from the wife and child of one of the masters, were the army officers who had been aboard the *Matunga*. As they held commissioned rank in the military they were accorded staterooms above deck.

On 13 August the two ships slowed as they approached the jungle-clad island of Waigeo, which was separated from the Dutch part of New Guinea (now West Papua) by the narrow Dampier Strait. The seaplane was lowered into the water and despatched to make sure that no other ships were in the vicinity. The *Wolf* then led the way through a narrow entrance into a long sheltered arm of water forming a safe natural harbour. The two ships moored alongside each other and the Germans wasted no time moving cargo and coal from the *Matunga*, while the remaining members of her crew were taken aboard the *Wolf*. The heat was intolerable, as much for the indolent (by force of circumstance) prisoners as for the Germans who, stripped down to just shorts and shoes, toiled under the merciless sun. There was not a breath of wind. At night the prisoners were sent below into what Captain Donaldson described as 'an atmosphere reeking with the smell of new paint flavoured by tobacco smoke, and a temperature bordering on Hell'.

Nerger had no intention of allowing a repetition of the escape at Sunday Island by permitting the prisoners to sleep on deck as they had been doing over the previous few nights at sea. This island, unlike the Kermadecs, was known to be inhabited, and so the risks of his presence being betrayed to the enemy were much greater. During the daytime a rope barrier was strung along the deck about a metre from the railings, outside which armed sailors patrolled so that no prisoner could slip overboard without being noticed. These sentries were doubled when Nerger heard rumours of a planned breakout, and the ship's lights were kept on all night. The heat, the hard work and the fears of escape all served to make the Germans tense and nervous.

The tension produced a wild scare among the German sailors one night, although the first the prisoners knew about it was when they were awakened at 11.00 pm by firing and shouting on the deck above. As Nerger rushed on to the deck to find out what was happening his men called out 'Prisoners overboard. There they are swimming.' Searchlights blazed out over the water, star shells exploded in the sky. More or more 'prisoners' were seen in the water by the overwrought Germans, so many that they must have believed most of the crews below had made it over the side. The sailors fired wildly as they thought they saw movement. As Nerger later wrote of the incident:

Rumours ran like wildfire from man to man, increasing as they spread. If the first man talked of one prisoner, the second talked of six, the third ten, and the fourth already saw them swimming in the water; the fifth fired away madly with the machine-gun.

The prisoners were able to see the searchlight beam through the hatch which, as a minor concession to the unbearable heat, Nerger had permitted to be left open. Then they saw the flares explode and heard the rattle of the machine-gun. The lights went on and German officers with revolvers, and sailors with rifles came down to count the two hundred men. All, naturally, were present and accounted for. The only victims of all this hysteria, apart from German self-respect, were the hawser lines holding the *Wolf* and the *Matunga* together and several crocodiles taken for escaping Allied seamen.

While it might have seemed funny to Nerger and the prisoners later, it was certainly a symptom of the growing unrest among the *Wolf's* crew. They had been at sea for almost eight months, during which time they had called at no port, their only contact with land being the bleak bay on Sunday Island and now this humid strip of water surrounded by dense jungle. During most of the time since leaving Germany they had to make do with dreary food and although from time to time stocks had been replenished — a huge amount of beer had been aboard *Matunga* — the monotony was oppressive. Nor could the men of the *Wolf* take all that much pride in their achievements. So far they had captured only nine ships, hardly more than one a month, and some of those had been insignificant catches; including the *Matunga* they had accounted for only 22,080 tons of Allied shipping.

The *Emden*, which had been their model, sank eighteen merchant ships, one Russian and one French warship, and had totally disrupted enemy shipping in the Indian Ocean. Other raiders had also done better: the *Moewe* in the first three months of 1916 had sunk fifteen ships totalling more than 58,000 tons. Not that the *Wolf*'s crew had any way of knowing, but on her second cruise (she had left Germany a week before the *Wolf*) the *Moewe* had sunk, by the end of March 1917, twenty-five vessels, accounting for 125,730 tons of shipping.

Just how keenly any feeling of disappointment was experienced by the Germans is unknown. The account written by Nerger was published while the war was still on and that, plus the fact that he and his men had been treated like heroes, would have prevented any admission of weakness. Nerger's account is, generally, of a highly boastful nature.

With all these strains, there was the constant and growing pressure of having prisoners aboard and of the chance that at any moment a British or Japanese cruiser would appear over the horizon and blast the *Wolf* to pieces. As the raider lay in the bay on Waigeo Island, its wireless crackled all day with the noise of other ships in the area.

Everything of use aboard the *Matunga* had been taken off, including three horses which were slaughtered to provide fresh meat. Scurvy had already broken out aboard the ship and the vegetables that were found aboard the Burns Philp vessel were quickly used up. Once everything had been moved over to the *Wolf*, the *Matunga* was steamed for the last time, taken out to sea and the bomb fuses set. She went down to a 'bloody good riddance' from her chief engineer who would no longer have to face the problem of keeping her straining to make seven and a half knots.

Nerger now set course through the Moluccas group into the Banda Sea. On the night of 3 September the alarm bells rang. A warship had been sighted. Men rushed to their action stations, the clattering feet giving way to tense silence as the two ships closed. She was definitely a British cruiser, although which one was not known. The German guns were loaded and ready behind their hinged flaps. The *Wolf*, which had had a paint job at Waigeo, did not look anything out of the usual. At fifteen hundred metres the tension was unbearable. The warship did not even ask for the *Wolf's* identity; she just turned away. The most likely explanation is that the *Wolf* had met the *Psyche*. On 31 August the Australians had notified the British Admiralty they had established lookouts in Torres Strait to watch for any enemy shipping, supplementing the searches in the Solomon Sea already described. Admiral Grant, on hearing this, sent the *Psyche* and the *Fantome* from Singapore to assist with the patrols. The time of their despatch would place them north of Java near the *Wolf* when the near-encounter occurred. It is probable that the crew on the *Psyche* did not even see the *Wolf* which was travelling blacked-out (her original white superstructure had been painted over soon after leaving Germany).

The *Wolf*, ignoring other merchant ships which would have normally been captured and sunk, joined the shipping lanes in the South China Sea. Nerger was more interested in finishing his mining plan, and at night laid a further 107 mines near the Anambas Islands, 240 kilometres north-east of Singapore, and directly in the path of shipping traffic between Singapore and the harbours of China and Japan. As the mines tumbled overboard, both crew and prisoners were still uncertain of Nerger's next move, there having been rumours aboard that Nerger would intern his ship at a neutral port.

He had no intention of so doing. Nerger announced to the crew that the *Wolf* would now go back to Germany.

9

The *Wolf* goes home

AFTER DROPPING THE LAST OF his mines, Nerger turned around and retraced his route along the seas north of Java and Bali, passing back into the Indian Ocean through the narrow channel separating the islands of Lombok and Sumbawa. As the ship began to pitch in the open seas once again, the Germans relaxed. Their chances of being accosted by the enemy were much slighter here. But for the captain the never absent concern about coal was once again a niggling problem. Even the crawl speed of five knots which Nerger had ordered to conserve fuel meant the *Wolf* was consuming thirty tons of coal a day, and this rate doubled if he had to work up to full speed to avoid a suspicious ship or chase a victim. Fresh food was also running low and even the prisoners were hoping another ship would be caught soon. The only item in abundance was tobacco due to the consignment aboard the *Matunga* bound for New Guinea. Lighting up a pipe or cigarette was one of the few things the prisoners could do to break the monotony as the *Wolf* waddled over the vast, empty Indian Ocean.

For more than two weeks Nerger searched in vain. He was looking in the wrong place. Little merchant shipping was traversing the mid-ocean region; whenever there was a raider scare, ships kept, as much as possible, close to the shores of the ocean where at least they might stand a chance making a run to a nearby port. Just as he had wasted his time in the roaring forties looking for Australian wheat ships, now Nerger ambled aimlessly in the Indian Ocean. Von Müller on the *Emden* had had the happy knack of finding ships; Nerger did not.

It was only when *Wolf* turned toward the edges of the ocean he once again found prizes. It was near the Maldives, which the *Emden* had found to be good hunting grounds, that he found the traffic from the Red Sea which had no other way to go on its way to Colombo and Calcutta. On the morning of 26 September the seaplane, having taken two hours to be assembled, was sent up to survey the scene. As it landed some time later smoke was seen on the horizon. The Germans immediately jumped to the conclusion that it came from a British cruiser. There was near panic as they worked to winch the aircraft aboard, Nerger, according to one account, losing his cool on the boat deck where he 'yelled, cursed and danced like a madman', while his men tried to get the plane out of the sea.

A few hours later, the raider's captain, having once more put the seaplane into the air, was relieved to find that the smoke was not from a warship but from a merchantman. She turned out to be the 6,688-ton *Hitachi Maru*, carrying valuable general cargo (rubber, tin, coffee, silk and tinned crab) from Japan to Liverpool via Delagoa Bay in Portuguese East Africa. As the *Wolf* closed, the raider ran up the usual signal flags ordering the merchantman to stop and not send any wireless message. This was followed by the raising of the German battle ensign and a shot across the Japanese ship's bow. The *Hitachi Maru* replied by signalling that she was stopping as ordered, and then, giving three blasts on her whistle, indicated that she was going full astern.

What she was in fact doing was swinging on her starboard helm to bring her stern, where a 120-millimetre gun was positioned, in line with the German raider. Aboard the *Wolf*, a shiver of excitement went through the gun crews as they were ordered to aim and fire. Never before had this ship had to fight and Nerger well knew that he could not afford to sustain a hit from the Japanese gun. While the *Wolf* had considerable firepower, she had few of the defence mechanisms (such as fire control) that were found aboard a conventional warship. Four guns now belched fire at the *Hitachi Maru*, one of the shells killing the Japanese gun crew. Another bunch of men rushed to take their place, but a salvo from the *Wolf's* guns exploded around them before the gun could be fired. Meanwhile, the Japanese wireless operator was busy sending out distress signals; these continued until Captain Seizu Tominaga ordered him to stop. The Japanese captain realised he could not escape. While the *Hitachi Maru* could make fifteen knots it realised its predicament too late to elude the *Wolf's* guns and now twenty of his men lay dead or wounded. Not that the shooting from the raider had been that accurate; of the fifteen shells fired, at near point blank range, only four had hit their target.

The final decision to surrender came when *Wolfchen* dropped a bomb under the bows of the Japanese ship. As the *Hitachi Maru* stopped, her men were lowering boats and jumping over the side. The Japanese captain was obviously distressed by the death of his men. Tominaga at first refused to leave his ship, and when eventually taken across to the *Wolf* he kept to himself (the Japanese crew themselves were kept in a separate hold from the rest of the prisoners), brooding for weeks over the incident. When the *Wolf* was on the final leg of her journey home, passing through the icy waters near Iceland, Tominaga threw himself overboard into water which would have killed him almost instantly, leaving Nerger a letter that said, in effect, that he could not live with the thought that the members of his crew died during the futile battle with the German ship.

With the capture of the Japanese ship, *Wolf* had more than twenty nationalities among her prisoners; the *Hitachi Maru's* passenger list included Chinese, Indian, Portuguese and British travellers. Nerger had decided not to transfer any cargo because he wanted to get away as soon as possible in case the wireless message from the Japanese ship had been picked up and because he also wanted to take the vessel back with him to Germany. All the items of cargo would be most useful to the fatherland's stretched war economy. The canned crab would be a useful variation in his prisoners' diet, so much so that after several weeks of crab most of the prisoners vowed they would never eat it again as long as they lived. The Germans repaired the steering gear damaged by the shelling so the freighter could again get under way and the two ships took shelter in an atoll in the Maldives group where they re-arranged the prison accommodation and stores. Only 200 tonnes of coal were taken aboard the *Wolf* because Nerger did not want to run the Japanese vessel short of fuel if he was to take her home as a prize.

On 20 October, with most of the more recently acquired prisoners now aboard the Japanese ship, the two vessels got going again. The German vessel had already been out into the ocean to look for other ships which might provide the coal she so desperately needed. Meanwhile, the Japanese Government had became alarmed when the *Hitachi Maru* did not arrive at her next destination, and had asked the Royal Navy to search the Maldives where it was thought the ship might have been wrecked. But it was not until 21 November that a French cruiser arrived at the atoll and learned from the natives of the two ships which had been there some weeks before. By the time the British had their ships scouring the western reaches of the Indian Ocean, Nerger was well around into the Atlantic.

Nerger's inability to find more victims had left him with little choice: there was only enough coal now for one ship, and so he made for Cargados Reef, about 500 kilometres northeast of Mauritius, where he proceeded to strip the *Hitachi Maru*. The prisoners were brought back to the *Wolf* so that overcrowding was now worse than ever with 400 people in addition to the *Wolf's* 300-strong crew. For days the Germans toiled, while the seaplane was sent aloft each day to make sure that they would not be surprised by an unwelcome enemy warship. On 7 November the *Hitachi Maru*, with much of her valuable cargo still in her holds, was taken to sea and despatched to the bottom.

Yet only three days later Nerger had all the coal he wanted: nearly 7,000 tons of Delagoa Bay coal bound for the British at Colombo. It came to him aboard the 4,740 ton Spanish collier *Igotz Mendi*, an attractive light grey ship with a distinctive yellow funnel. Nerger took his new find back to the Cargados Reef, where he transferred only enough coal for immediate needs having decided to keep the Spanish collier with him and replenish coal into his own bunkers as required. He put the women prisoners, with their husbands, into the officers' quarters of the *Igotz Mendi*. The ship was to stay with the *Wolf* until early February when, detached to find her own way to Germany, she was wrecked near the Skaw lighthouse at the northern tip of Denmark. Upon their release by the Danes, the former prisoners were reported by Reuters as having complained about their treatment. The women said that the German prize crew aboard the collier had not been gentlemanly, that they had been closely guarded and had eaten little and bad food; even after the ship had become stranded and before they were released at the insistence of the Danes the Germans had refused them any concessions. Still, it was a long way from the headlines in the Sydney press of 'Barbarity on the *Wolf*'.

After refuelling from the *Igotz Mendi*, Nerger arranged to rendezvous with the collier in the Atlantic, and the two ships parted. Nerger now wanted to get home.

As he was heading back into the Atlantic on 30 November, a year to the day since the *Wolf* had left Kiel, he encountered the American barque *John H. Kirby* (1,321 tons) bound for Port Elizabeth in South Africa, out of New York with a load of 270 Ford motorcars for civilian use (not armoured cars as Nerger later claimed) and canned goods. Her food stores were taken and the sailing ship was sunk.

On 3 December the *Wolf* was once more in the South Atlantic and the cooler weather was a relief for the prisoners. It also helped restrain the spread of scurvy and typhoid. The latter was discovered among several Japanese prisoners and everyone on board was then inoculated; it was more difficult, however, to control the spread of scurvy. By mid-December there were twenty cases, all among men from the *Jumna* and *Wordsworth* who had by now been captive for nine months. On 14 December the French barque *Marechal Davout* (2,235 tons) was stopped, but she had no fresh fruit or vegetables aboard. She had sailed from Geelong with 3,500 tons of wheat for Dakar in French West Africa (now Senegal). Both ship and cargo were sunk. One thing she did provide was a large quantity of wine which added a little joy to the Christmas Day celebrations in the prisoners' quarters.

Nerger had arranged to meet his collier at Trinidad Island, a Brazilian possession in the mid Atlantic (and not to be confused with the country of the same name in the West Indies).

The Germans thought the island to be uninhabited. Trinidad Island had featured prominently in the life of an earlier raider, the *Cap Trafalgar* (The 18,300-ton liner had been in Buenos Aires at the outbreak of war. She headed for Trinidad Island where she met up with the *Eber*, a gunboat and the cargo steamer *Steiemark*, both of which were more suited to the calm, steamy waters of the estuaries and rivers of German West Africa than to battling across the Atlantic. The cruiser *Dresden* had earlier met a collier at the island to recoal on her way to Cape Horn, so it seemed a useful place to rendezvous. On 14 September 1914, without herself having captured a ship, the luxury *Cap Trafalgar* was sunk by the *Carmania* near Trinidad Island with the loss of sixteen lives. The remainder of the crew of this short-lived auxiliary raider were interned in Argentina.)

By the time Nerger came along the island was in fact inhabited, by Brazilian troops as it turned out. He found out just in time when he intercepted a wireless message from the Brazilian admiralty to the military governor on the island.

He was thus forced to coal out on the persistent swell of the Atlantic Ocean, an operation difficult enough at any time but which was made worse by the fact that the *Igotz Mendi* rolled badly even in slight seas. In these conditions the Spanish ship was a nightmare to handle. Slowly the two ships came together and were made fast. Then it began. Each time the Spanish collier dipped she crashed against the raider's waterline, sending sickening blows through both ships. On and on it went: the sailors clambered around swinging nets full of coal sacks from one ship to the other, the coal spilling all over the *Wolf's* deck. That did not matter; all Nerger wanted was enough to get home. Down below the prisoners were thrown about each time the ships hit and they could hear the water coming in through the damaged plates. The Germans became extremely anxious. Too much of this pounding would start leaks which they would be unable to control. But Nerger had to have his coal. Eventually it was done, and everyone sighed with relief as the collier was untied and it pulled away. It took four days' work to made rudimentary repairs to the *Wolf* which would see her home.

Nerger, by this time, was no longer much interested in further plunder. He already had a rather inflated view of the effects of his cruise, and felt that he had done enough. But, on 4 January, the Norwegian four-master *Storebror* of 2,091 tons crossed his path. She was a neutral ship which should have protected her, and she was also in ballast (bound from Lourenco Marques to Montevideo) which made her worthless as a prize. His initial inclination was to leave her alone, but a fear began niggling in Nerger's mind that the Norwegian sailing ship might pass information about the black ship it had seen on to the British, leading Nerger to turn about and catch the Norwegian. The knowledge that she was a former British ship gave Nerger the flimsy shred of legality he needed to justify seizing and sinking the Storebror.

Once more he coaled from the *Igotz Mendi* — producing more battered hull plates — and at last it was time for the final run home. In some ways this was to be the *Wolf's* sternest test. She had to run both the British blockade and survive the filthiest weather of which the North Atlantic was capable. At one stage the *Wolf* was in danger of foundering. Below decks the prisoners and their belongings were thrown from one side to the other. The northwest gales were flinging hail and snow and the waves were battering the sides. The plates which had already been damaged sprang leaks once again. There were by now fifty cases of scurvy, and the end of the voyage could not come too soon for the wretched prisoners.

Nerger's first plan was to make his way through the Denmark Strait separating Greenland and Iceland. There he found pack ice.

The prisoners knew that the ship was in ice-strewn water only by the noise of the floes scraping along the hull. The *Wolf* zigzagged in a futile attempt to find a path through the ice. Nerger had no alternative but to go south of Iceland, knowing that British warships would be there in great numbers to combat the German U-boat menace. On 14 February the *Wolf* sailed into Norwegian territorial waters and stayed within the three mile limit until, passing Denmark, she slid into German waters and dropped anchor.

After the momentary disbelief on board German warships as the raider passed by — she had had no contact with the German Navy for fourteen months — the *Wolf* was welcomed tumultuously in a Germany which badly needed some good news. Nerger and his crew were feted. After a week to clean up the ship, they sailed her into Kiel on 24 February, past fifteen battleships and battle-cruisers and many smaller navy ships, many with their bands playing, all with sailors lining the rails cheering the ordinary looking black steamer. She dropped anchor just a few hundred metres from the *Moewe*.

Wolf reaches her home port after being at sea for fifteen months and having steamed more than 100,000km. [Paul Schmalenbach Collection]

As was by now the custom in Germany — the Kaiser had made a mockery of the Iron Cross with its profligate bestowal since 1914 — all the *Wolf's* crew were presented with the medal. Then they all travelled to Berlin and marched through cheering crowds. The captain and his men were separated and posted to different parts of the navy, and the *Wolf* was quickly forgotten.

After the war the *Wolf* was taken as reparation by the French and worked as the Messageries Maritimes cargo steamer *Antinous* until going to the breaker's yard in 1931.

10

The Sea Devil

ON 25 OCTOBER 1917 it was officially announced from Washington there were two armed German raiders in the South Pacific. Allied warships, the announcement said, were searching for them. The United States Navy had learned of the existence of the second raider from the commander at Tutuila, American Samoa, when four American sailors arrived there. The men told the U.S. naval authorities at the Pago Pago base that the *Seeadler* had captured their vessels and that the raider had later been stranded and abandoned in the Tahitian group.

At this time there was still great confusion about the fate of the *Wairuna*. An inquiry had been held in New Zealand but the only alternatives that could be offered by way of explanation were the normal hazards of the sea, or an internal explosion (still very much in vogue as a reason for unexplained sinkings) or the work of a raider. The news of the *Seeadler* seemed to fit this latter theory, and the Americans assumed that this raider was responsible. The New Zealanders jumped to the same conclusion, and it took some time for the captain of the *Seeadler*, when in the custody of the New Zealand Army, to persuade them he had never even heard of the missing Union company ship let alone being able to claim responsibility for sinking her.

The raider captain, Count Felix von Luckner — the 'Sea Devil' as he would come to be known — was not the sort of man who would lie. His every act was dictated by the conventions of seamanlike chivalry. His early training and experience on sailing vessels surpassed that of most other German naval officers so, although he lacked the seniority in 1916 to rate a command of his own, he was the obvious choice when the Imperial German Navy decided to commission a sailing ship as a commerce raider. He had begun his sea-going career as a fo'c'sle hand, then passed the examination for an officer's ticket in the merchant marine and finally joined the navy. As noted earlier, the navy was very much the second choice for a military career in Germany. But it was ideal for those who could not stomach the demands of life in the Prussian-dominated army officer corps. Germany had possessed a national navy only since the Empire was founded in 1871, and it had relatively little tradition. It was the darling of the middle classes of the new Germany; not of the Junkers of East Prussia.

Von Luckner's early rumbustious life at sea certainly would have knocked any pomposity out of the young von Luckner, and he was just thirty-four when given command of the *Seeadler*. His career in the navy since 1910 had included service aboard the cruiser *Panther* sent to German Cameroons in West Africa, the battleship *Kronprinz* during the Battle of Jutland and as gunnery officer on the first voyage of the commerce raider the *Moewe*. He was a popular officer, and was well liked by his men when he took command of the *Seeadler*. Those who were captured by him all spoke well of von Luckner.

The choice of a sailing ship for raider operations was an inspired one. It solved the one major headache now that all the German colonies had been lost and the *etappen* no longer existed. A sailing ship required no coal nor would it look out of place. There were still plenty of sailing ships on the high seas (the huge square-rigged, four-masted barques would be used in the South Australia wheat trade until 1939).

The ship chosen was the *Pass of Balmaha*. She had been captured by a U-boat in 1915, an American ship carrying cotton from New York to Archangel in what was then still Tsarist Russia. The ship had been owned originally by the River Plate Shipping Company and was built in 1878 by Duncan and Company of Scotland. The *Pass of Balmaha* weighed 1,602 tons gross, she was eighty-three metres long and had a draught of 5.5 metres.

Von Luckner knew that he could not rely on sail alone. While sails released him from complete dependence on coal, the wind was not reliable enough. The raider would have to be able to maintain complete and total manoeuvrability so she could make her escape if she encountered an enemy naval ship. The answer was to install a diesel engine, a type of propulsion not yet considered sufficiently reliable on its own but certainly adequate in an auxiliary role.

For weeks workmen had toiled aboard the ship reshaping everything except for the hull and the masts. In addition to the engines, room had to be found for the fuel tanks and for large water tanks which would provide not only for extended duration at sea but for the many prisoners the Germans intended to capture. Access to the engine room — as one of the holds had now become — was by means of a door at the back of a cupboard. The Germans realised that there was every chance that they would be stopped and inspected by the British and the discovery of an engine aboard a sailing ship would arouse great suspicion, but the door to it was not easily spotted. Apart from accommodating a diesel engine, the space below decks was fitted out with hammocks for captured crews, and three-bunk cabins for their officers; these cabins had stocks of French and English books with which the prisoners would while away the long days and nights of captivity. Below decks would also serve, during the run through the British blockade, as a hiding place for part of the crew, should the ship be stopped and searched because the British would never believe that a cargo carrying clipper needed a crew of sixty-five men. One thing that would make an inspection by the Royal Navy of the area below deck impossible, or at least impracticable, was to load the deck with timber; it was common for lumber ships to have a cargo of logs or planks piled over the hatch covers. The vessel's ordnance (two 105-millimetre guns and 400 rounds of ammunition, plus small arms) were also stowed below.

While the *Pass of Balmaha* was undergoing the radical changes needed to fit her out as a raider she was temporarily named the *Walter*, the explanation being given to any curious German that she was being equipped as a cadet-training ship, which provided a plausible reason for the huge number of bunks and hammocks being installed, not to mention the engine.

Once at sea, the ship would have to adopt that status of a neutral. Von Luckner's first choice was to impersonate a Norwegian clipper named *Maletta* which bore an uncanny resemblance to his own ship. Unfortunately, the *Maletta* was also in northern waters at about the time during which von Luckner was due to sail, so that prevented him using her name. Instead an entirely fictitious name, *Irma*, was bestowed for the purposes of fooling the British should the vessel be stopped and searched. Several members of the crew had been chosen because they could speak Norwegian.

As far as the German Navy records were concerned their new sailing ship was called the *Seeadler* — *Sea Eagle* — an identity she would assume once past the blockade.

An artist's impression of Seeadler *under full sail.* [Alexander Turnbull Library]

The initial disguise required more than superficial considerations such as painting a false name on the stern and providing a matching ship's log to support the ruse. Timber, complete with Norwegian markings, was loaded, and papers forged to show that the vessel was carrying its cargo from Copenhagen to Melbourne. All the deck machinery and all the instruments, including the barometers and the compasses, were stamped with the names of Norwegian companies. The crew's quarters were decorated with Norwegian scenes and Norwegian papers were left lying about. Norwegian and Danish food was used to stock the galley and Norwegian clothing had been bought for the crew.

Not all the men had to be part of the facade. Those whose role it was to hide below deck if the ship was stopped needed to play no active part in the disguise. The Germans had carefully selected twenty-three sailors who could speak Norwegian and these were the men who would be seen by any British force that came aboard. Each of the men, along with four officers (the total of twenty-seven being the typically sized crew for a vessel such as this) was given a Norwegian name and birthplace and was ordered to study as much as possible about the particular town so that he could answer any reasonable questions about the place. They would not be likely to fool a Norwegian, but then it would not be the Norwegians who would be stopping the *Seeadler*.

The deception became even more detailed. Letters were written in Norwegian so that each man's locker contained correspondence from 'home' and photographs of loved ones were stamped on the back with the names of photographers in the towns whence they were supposed to come. The men were repeatedly quizzed and tested to make certain there were no mistakes, omissions or inconsistencies in their stories. If he gave the wrong age for a child or the incorrect occupation for his father, a crewman would be punished. Von Luckner knew that British patrols in the North Sea were being constantly stiffened. If a Royal Navy officer walked into the mess area his suspicions had to be immediately allayed by the piles of Norwegian books and records and by the photos of the Norwegian king. As a final touch one of the youngest of the sailors was issued with women's clothes so that he could play the part of the captain's wife.

They sailed four days before Christmas of 1916, three weeks after the *Wolf*. The *Seeadler* had to pause in the Heligoland Bight, north of the Friesian Islands, in order to collect a load of timber. This could not be done in port without destroying her cover as a training ship. Then the Germans set course north and west across the North Sea, von Luckner planning to skirt around the northern tip of Scotland. The weather turned bad with raging south-westerly gales which drove the *Seeadler* far off course, but von Luckner dared not use his auxiliary engines even though they would have been of great use. Another ship could come upon the scene any moment in those seas and it would be too risky to be sighted ploughing through the waves with little or no sail rigged. On Christmas morning the *Seeadler* had battled the odds in surviving three days of extremely bad weather and high seas and had made it to a position midway between the Faroe Islands and Iceland when a large steamship came into view out of the rain.

Von Luckner met the British blockade in the form of the armed merchant cruiser *Patia*, part of the Royal Navy's northern patrol which guarded the seas north of the Shetlands. The *Patia* signalled the sailing ship to heave to and await a boat. The German-speaking section of the crew rushed below, closing off the doors behind them to wait in silence while the British came aboard. They were armed and ready to attack the boarders if the deception was unsuccessful. It was not a full boarding party, consisting of only two officers who looked around and inspected the ship's papers. As no account survives of the British record of this inspection — no doubt one of many the officers carried out and at the time they would have seen no especial significance in it — what transpired is unclear, and even the official war history had to be content with von Luckner's version of the story. According to that, two Englishmen came aboard and made their way, with von Luckner, to the master's cabin where the slim young sailor was sitting with his blond wig and dress on. Von Luckner explained that his 'wife' was suffering from toothache and so was unable to do much more than mumble. The German captain spoke in a mixture of broken English and Norwegian. Piles of wet clothing and papers had been strewn around the cabin to lend credence to the German's account of the dreadful storm that had pushed him off course. For a moment on two separate occasions it looked as if the jig might be up. First, the British asked why, according to its logs, the ship had been delayed, when the *Seeadler* had in fact been anchored in the Heligoland Bight taking on its cargo and waiting for final clearance to sail. Von Luckner replied that he had been waiting to avoid German raiders who would certainly want to seize his valuable cargo. The other moment of tension came when the British, back in their boat, were drifting aft along *Seeadler*'s side. As von Luckner looked over the rail he could see the propeller quite clearly in the water and reasoned that so would the British if they bothered to look down, so he swung a rope over for them to grab and pull their boat forward. The British kept their eyes on the rope, and did not see the tell-tale propeller.

Once the *Patia* was out of sight, the Germans pulled on their naval uniforms and celebrated Christmas Day in the knowledge that they were through the British blockade. Two days later they mounted the guns and ditched the cargo of timber overboard.

The *Seeadler* was ready to go raiding.

While in the Atlantic, Von Luckner would capture twelve vessels in all. The first was the British *Gladys Royal* of 3,333 tons and bound from Cardiff to Buenos Aires with a load of good Welsh coal — what a prize she would have been for any raider other than the *Seeadler!* The sailing ship signalled the steamer asking for a chronometer check. The *Gladys Royal* slowed and then came what would be the usual procedure from the German ship — the order to stop being signalled, the German ensign replacing the Norwegian flag and then a shot across the bows. But this time the British captain decided to make a run for it, hoisting his Union Jack and stopping only after the third shell had passed over his funnel.

After she was stripped of useful stores, the merchantman was sunk by explosives.

The next day it was the turn of the *Lundy Island* (3,156 tons) en route from Martinique to France with a consignment of sugar. She was shelled and sunk after her crew had been taken aboard the *Seeadler*. Others followed: the French barque *Charles Gounod* (2,242 tons) carrying corn to Bordeaux; the Canadian three-master *Perce* (371 tons) carrying dried fruit from Halifax to Santos, the Brazilian port serving the city of Sao Paulo; the French barque *Antonin* (3,132 tons) carrying saltpetre to Brest; and the *Buenos Aires*, a 1,087-ton Italian sailing vessel (Italy having entered the war against the central powers in 1915). Seeadler had the advantage of being able to get close to its intended quarry without the other vessel's captain being alerted to danger: the last type of ship that would arouse the suspicions of any master alert for commerce raiders was a handsome sailing clipper. Many a steamer captain had served under sail in his early days so that when the *Seeadler* made her approach broadsides and asked for a time signal or a request for a geographical position, both of which were common requests from sailing vessels, no one thought anything much amiss — until, that is, they were told to stop and not use their wireless, by which time the raider had her guns trained on the victim.

The Germans had begun their raiding activity around Rocas Island off the north-east coast of Brazil and generally concentrated on the stretch of ocean where the Atlantic was narrowest between West Africa and South America, a stretch of ocean always busy with merchant shipping.

The *Pinmore* (2,431 tons) was von Luckner's next victim, captured on 19 February 1917. On the morning of 19 February the mate of the British barque was on the poop when he saw another sailing vessel approaching. He reported to the captain that she was flying Norwegian colours and signal flags. Closer examination through the glasses aroused Captain John Mullen's suspicions as the approaching ship seemed to be manoeuvring strangely, and by the time the *Seeadler* dropped her sails and was seen to be moving under power it was too late. The Norwegian flag came down and the German ensign shot up in its place.

'Stop instantly, or I will fire on your ship' came the signal from the *Seeadler*. There was a light wind running and Mullen knew he had no chance of outrunning a powered ship. Suddenly the Germans, seeing that *Pinmore* was making no apparent effort to stop, fired one of their guns at the British ship's foremast, missing by about six metres. It was not until *Seeadler* had fired another shot, which just cleared the cross-jack yard (the lowest on the mizzen-mast), that Mullen decided he had better obey the order to stop. As the raider came closer, the British crew could see that there were a number of machine guns and rifles pointed at them.

A few minutes later a nine-metre motorboat put out from the *Seeadler* carrying a prize officer and ten men. The prize officer saluted as he boarded the *Pinmore* and ordered Mullen to abandon ship, that he had been instructed to sink the ship and was about to place bombs in the hull. Everything was done in a quiet and orderly manner and the men were allowed to take their personal effects with them, a second motor boat coming from the *Seeadler* to take the two lifeboats in tow. Captain Mullen was allowed to stay aboard his vessel until the last moment and a launch was sent to bring him to the raider. The Germans did seize all the stores, but they shared all their food with the prisoners.

'Why did you not stop?', von Luckner asked as Mullen stepped on to the deck of *Seeadler*. Mullen did not record his reply, but after his release he described von Luckner as 'a true sport' and his treatment of the prisoners as 'fair and square'. Quarters, with electric light, were provided aft for officers while the men were accommodated below deck forward. The prisoners, like those from previously captured ships, were told that as long as they behaved themselves everything would be all right, but that if they caused trouble aboard ship they could expect no quarter. It is obvious from a number of incidents that von Luckner had a sharp sense of humour and could tell a plausible tall story. Mullen fully believed that the *Seeadler* was equipped with poisonous gases which were connected to the prisoners' quarters and that von Luckner, simply by pressing a button fitted just under his bunk, could asphyxiate all the prisoners should they at any time show signs of hostility.

After the exigent weather and sea conditions north of Britain and the Faroe Islands, von Luckner picked up a fair wind for his voyage south. Now, well away from waters off Norway, he could finally assume the identity of the *Maletta*.

Meanwhile, by the early weeks of January 1917, the British had checked out the details of the sailing ship which had been inspected on Christmas Day by the armed merchant cruiser *Patia* and they knew something was amiss although still not sure it was a raider they had missed. Von Luckner, too, knew he would not fool the British so easily a second time especially now that the timber had been jettisoned. With the hatchways uncovered, any efficient boarding party would have demanded they be opened for inspection.

But another development played into von Luckner's hands. Britain's ninth cruiser squadron had hitherto been patrolling a wide area out from Madeira and the Canary Islands, but these ships were by now kept fully employed escorting troop transports from India, Australia and New Zealand which were sailing via the Cape of Good Hope until they reached the safety of the channel ports. Coaling for the Royal Navy was now restricted to either Freetown in Sierra Leone, or Dakar in French West Africa. The *Seeadler* was able to proceed unchallenged beyond those sea lanes used by the convoys.

The prison quarters continued to fill. On 26 February 1917 it was the turn of the *British Yeoman* (1,992 tons), a Canadian sailing ship. The next day von Luckner caught another sailing ship, the French barque *La Rochefoucauld* (2,244 tons) carrying saltpetre, and on 5 March another saltpetre cargo aboard the French *Dupleix* (2,250 tons) was sent to the bottom thus depriving the French munitions industry of valuable raw materials.

It was not until 11 March that von Luckner was to capture another steamer. She was the 3,681 ton *Horngarth*, carrying Argentine corn to England. By the time he captured the French barque *Cambronne* (1,869 tons) which was carrying nitrates, von Luckner had 260 prisoners. He could not continue to add to the prison holds, which he would have to do if he kept on raiding and capturing ships. He was also aware that the *Seeadler* would soon have to move to a new hunting ground, as British naval intelligence would by now be alerted to his presence by the non-arrival of all the captured ships.

He decided, therefore, not to sink the *Cambronne*, but to use her to evacuate the prisoners; he would then make his way via Cape Horn into the Pacific. The Germans dumped much of the *Cambronne's* cargo of nitrate overboard to make room for the captured crews, which were, by this time, a mixed bunch of English, French, Danes, Italians, Chinese Malays and West Indians. Fearing the *Cambronne* might make Rio de Janiero, the nearest port, before he was far enough away, von Luckner ordered that the topmasts be removed in order to force her to sail much more slowly. He placed her in charge of Captain Mullen and presented him with a British ensign to fly. He paid £800 pounds to the group of prisoners who had carried out some work while on board, such as sail making and rigging. He then assembled Mullen and other senior officers in the saloon and, over glasses of wine, wished them good luck and a safe passage to their destination. He handed Mullen a photograph of his family, which had been rescued from Mullen's cabin on the *Pinmore* by the German prize crew.

When she reached Rio, the *Cambronne* was handed back to her French captain and the tricolour raised again. Mullen told the British naval authorities in Rio that the *Seeadler* had a powerful wireless aboard and that von Luckner constantly monitored wireless traffic between British warships in order to avoid meeting them.

The British had received news five days earlier that a raider was active near St Paul Rocks, a Brazilian outcrop on the equator. One vital piece of information brought by the released prisoners was that von Luckner had many charts of Cape Horn. The British had seven ships on the Pacific coast of South America. Of these, the cruisers *Lancaster* and *Otranto* were ordered to leave Peru and sail south to intercept the raider. They were also to be joined by the armed merchant cruiser *Orbita* which was berthed at the northern Chilean port of Mejillones at that time.

While von Luckner was holding a memorial service over the spot near the Falkland Islands where Admiral von Spee's East Asiatic Squadron had been sunk more than two years previously, the British were racing down the other side of South America in a desperate bid to find him. His luck continued to hold. So foul was the weather that he was forced to sail south of Cape Horn by about 190 kilometres. The British were meanwhile working on the assumption he would cling to the cape as he rounded into the Pacific. The *Orbita* had been ordered to patrol off the cape, but in fact kept on going right past Staten Island (now Islas de los Estados) off the tip of Argentina. On that day the *Seeadler* was passing far to the south; if the *Orbita* had stopped at the Horn and patrolled there she might conceivably have caught the German ship. The *Otranto* and the *Lancaster* were still racing down the coast, having passed Valdivia but were still far from the Horn. Had the wind dropped and allowed von Luckner to drive northwards he might have been snared by these ships, but the wind did not abate and he was forced to continue beating westward. By 19 April 1917 the *Seeadler* was well clear of the British cruisers. Two days later he swung her north.

Over the following days the winds dropped, the seas no longer beat hard against her side, and the *Seeadler* was at large in the Pacific Ocean.

11

You Left the Door Open

BY THE TIME *SEEADLER* had reached the doldrums of the equatorial Pacific, the United States had joined the war. The Germans knew that a great many American sailing ships were active in the Pacific, particularly around the islands of Polynesia and Melanesia. However, in five weeks of searching, all they could manage to find were three small ships sailing between the United States and Australia.

It is difficult to understand why, at this stage of the war, the German navy should see any point in raiding shipping on such a small scale halfway around the world. It is true that in the early months of 1917 Germany made official and semi-official statements to the effect that they would expect any peace agreements to include the return of their colonies — and it was the African colonies they had mostly in mind. Those in the Pacific would scarcely have been missed.

But there was another factor that raises questions about the persistence with the Pacific raiding strategy: the Atlantic should clearly have been a greater priority. Two-thirds of Britain's food was imported, and during wartime almost all of its had to be shipped via the Atlantic Ocean. Now that the United States was in the war, the sea traffic flowing from ports on the eastern seaboard presented a substantial target for the German U-boats. These submarines had already sealed off the Mediterranean to the British, which is why transport convoys from Australasia and India were being sent around the Cape of Good Hope. Successful attacks by U-38 on Allied shipping at Funchal in Madeira had been the first step in the German navy's plan to isolate French West Africa and Morocco, a valuable source of men and raw materials for the Western Front. As the Germans built larger submarines, so they were able to extend their operations closer to North America.

What effect a sailing ship raider preying on the Pacific trade would have on the war in Europe is difficult to imagine. It was hardly even likely to divert warships from convoy duty, as the British and Japanese still had sufficient ships left in the Pacific to hunt down a raider.

The three small ships which von Luckner eventually managed to capture in the Pacific Ocean were the *A. B. Johnson* (539 tonnes) sailing from San Francisco to Newcastle with plenty of fresh food aboard; the *R. C. Slade* (686 tonnes) carrying copra to Sydney and the *Manila* (745 tonnes) bound for Newcastle in Australia. The American sailors were still indignant about their capture months later after they were back in Allied hands, the master of the *R. C. Slade* talking in terms of 'undisguised piracy'; as the *Seeadler* had approached, a shell had been fired across the schooner's bows, quickly followed by two more.

Von Luckner, by this time, was running short of food and fresh water, and scurvy had broken out. The men, like those on the *Wolf* in the Tasman Sea, were weary and exhausted after seven months at sea without any landfall to break the monotony. The problem: where could they land without giving themselves away? All the islands, uninhabited or not, were either occupied or patrolled by ships belonging to Allied colonial administrations.

Von Luckner finally plumped for Mopelia, a small atoll in the Society Islands. Situated 450 kilometres from Papeete, and inhabited by only a handful of Polynesian labourers left there to harvest copra for the company which leased the island, it was visited once every three months by the ship which came to collect that copra. The atoll is circular, and about ten kilometres across with a deep and sheltered lagoon. The passage into the lagoon, however, was not deep enough for the *Seeadler* to negotiate safely. Most of the men, therefore, went ashore by boat to gather food and water while their ship lay at anchor outside the reef. Mopelia proved to be the bountiful haven they had hoped for.

On 2 August 1917 all seemed well. The crew and prisoners found the break ashore just the tonic they needed. They lay around, basking in the sun. It seemed perfect, until — according to von Luckner's account — a bulge was noticed on the horizon. This version has that, almost without warning, a strong wind blew up and the bulge was soon seen to be a small tidal wave — and it was headed straight for the *Seeadler*. This appears to have been an almost totally fictional account of the episode. It is now believed Seeadler dragged its anchor in heavy seas. The Germans still aboard the ship started the engine in an attempt to get under way and put some distance between themselves and the sharp coral reef but they were too late. The hull was stoved-in beyond repair and the masts came down in a tangle of rigging.

The Germans salvaged what was left. This amounted to two ship's boats, provisions, and firearms. Von Luckner had saved many of his navigation instruments. There was sufficient canvas and

enough spars to provide some shelter ashore; the American pris-
oners named their area Broadway; the Germans Potsdamerplatz.
Von Luckner, his sense of humour still intact, proclaimed that his
Seeadlerdorf ought not to be considered the last German colony.

*Sailors from an unidentified Australian naval vessel board the wreck of
the* Seeadler *at Mopelia Island some time after von Luckner's capture.*
[Australian War Memorial A995]

Von Luckner was down but not out. He decided to take to the ocean in one of the motor boats and try to capture a schooner, aboard which he would return to Mopelia, pick up the rest of his men and prisoners, and resume his career as a commerce raider. What followed was an extraordinary feat of seamanship. The largest of the motor boats, named *Kronprinzessin Cecilie*, was fitted out with masts and hurriedly sewn sails, guns and plenty of provisions. He chose five men, and on 22 August 1917 sailed off into the blue haze of the ocean horizon.

After sailing for days across the empty sea, they sighted land. It was the island of Atiu in the Cook Islands group (which had been annexed in 1900 by New Zealand as part of Britain's response to German colonial acquisition in the Pacific). After sailing into the harbour they told the New Zealand resident there they were Dutch-American sailors crossing the Pacific as part of a wager. The resident gave them sufficient fresh supplies to take them on to another island in the Cooks, Aitutaki, where the New Zealand resident was not quite so sure of his visitors (who now posing as Norwegians). The resident was clearly suspicious but, in spite of the urgings of the locals to arrest the six men, he had no means of so doing, being unarmed himself and well aware of the guns and grenades aboard the strange boat.

While they now had food, the Germans still had no schooner. They set course for Fiji, which as one of the major island groups of the South Pacific was much more likely to provide the ship which they so desperately needed. By the time they reached Fiji they had covered 3,700 kilometres of ocean in an open boat. They were completely exhausted when, on 21 September, they anchored at the Fijian Island of Wakaya. They had battled sun and wind, and endured scurvy and blistered faces.

The people they encountered on Wakaya, among them a schooner captain, treated the newcomers with some friendliness, ostensibly believing von Luckner's story that they were ship-wrecked sailors from a Norwegian ship. However one sceptic set off for the police station at Levuka, the old capital of Fiji before the British chose Suva for their colonial administration. A party of Fijian policemen led by Sub-Inspector H.C. Hills set out in the inter-island steamer *Amra* to question the new arrivals. As *Amra* approached Wakaya a boat was seen heading for the harbour entrance. Hills had a boat lowered and, with his unarmed men, put toward the German boat and cut across its bows.

Hills stood up in the boat and shouted: 'I call on you to surrender, in the name of the King.' He made no attempt to draw his revolver. 'Who are you?', responded von Luckner in his excellent English. 'Who do you belong to?' 'I call on you to surrender,' Hills repeated. 'I do not wish to parley.'

There was some hesitation while Sub-Inspector Hills explained that failure to surrender would mean that he would order the *Amra* (which was actually unarmed) to use her gun to blow the Germans out of the water. Von Luckner thereupon surrendered and did not discover that he had been tricked, that in fact Amra had no guns at all, until he was safely aboard her and in custody. 'We did not come this distance to be captured by an unarmed boat', the Count told his captors, somewhat chagrined. The prisoners were taken to Suva, where they were disembarked at night to avoid any trouble. A number of people did spot the Germans as they were being marched to Suva Gaol and shouted abuse at them. War fever spread quickly through the administration after von Luckner, having given a summary of what had happened to his ship, stated that there were other boats from the *Seeadler* at large, but that he was not prepared to say where they were. The Governor issued a proclamation to the effect that invasion was possible and search parties were sent out over Viti Levu, the main island of Fiji, to look for more Germans.

Meanwhile, back on Mopelia, the Germans were beginning to despair as, day by day, there was no sign of their captain and the schooner he had promised to capture. On 1 September Leutnant Kling, who had been left in charge, was listening to the wireless (each day the Germans monitored Pago Pago, Honolulu and Papeete for news) and picked up a message about the missing *A.B. Johnson*. It was clear that the Americans and their allies would soon begin to search the area, and once the other two ships also became overdue at their destinations, they would realise that the German raider last heard of in the South Atlantic was now at work in Polynesia. Kling had no desire to end up in a prison camp. On the other hand he could not risk a sea journey in the boat that von Luckner had left behind; it was by far the less seaworthy of the two craft.

On the morning of 5 September sails appeared over the horizon. It was the island trader the *Lutece* (128 tonnes) out of Papeete, a fore-and aft-rigged schooner which had been built in Auckland in 1885 and had served as the German-owned *Gauloise* until seized by the French in 1914. Now Kling — although he did not know her history — was about to reclaim what had been German property.

Kling acted quickly, rowing out to the schooner, climbing aboard and taking the ship at the point of a gun, exactly what von Luckner had planned to do. The lieutenant had momentary visions of repeating von Mücke's great escape by sailing around the Horn and into the Atlantic and then running the blockade back to Germany. There was no question that they would take along their American prisoners — to whom the master, crew and three passengers aboard *Lutece* had been added — simply because the ship was not big enough. He did, however, leave supplies and a boat, but took the wireless and all the arms. Setting sail for the coast of South America, Kling soon discovered the schooner was taking a great deal of water. He decided to put in at Easter Island, where the ship went aground. For some time the Germans lived in freedom on the island, but eventually they were transferred to Chile where they were interned for the remainder of the war.

Meanwhile, Captain Smith from the *A.B. Johnson* realised that something had to be done, that the former captives could not just sit idly on Mopelia. His first attempt, with three other American seamen, was to take the remaining boat and attempt to reach the nearest island, about 160 kilometres away. But they struck bad weather and returned, exhausted, to the atoll. Smith then carried out repairs to the boat and set sail for Pago Pago. He was carrying two sextants, a compass and enough provisions for a ten day journey. When, on 6 October 1917, he and his men sailed into the port at American Samoa he had almost equalled von Luckner's navigational feat.

He also alerted American authorities to the fact there were still forty-four sailors stranded on the island where Kling had left them. His account stated that the Germans had left them a quantity of bad flour, some sugar, butter, canned milk and some syrup and molasses. There were coconuts on the atoll, but these were usually eaten by rats before the humans could collect them. With Kling in internment in Chile and von Luckner, by this time, confined to a prisoner-of-war camp near Auckland, New Zealand it seemed that the end of the story of the *Seeadler* had come.

Von Luckner had other ideas.

Only he and the other officer from the *Seeadler*, Leutnant Carl Kircheiss, had been locked up on Motuihi Island in the Hauraki Gulf near Auckland. The island was being used to intern the Germans captured in Samoa. The other four *Seeadler* sailors were taken to Somes Island in Wellington Harbour. It had originally been intended to put the two officers on Somes, too, but the New Zealand authorities felt that it was reasonable to spare them from contact with the 'harder prisoners' at that camp.

The count had to find competent sailors to take the place of his other comrades. He was entitled to a batman of his own choice and thus managed to get one of the men back from Somes Island. Fortunately, among the prisoners at Motuihe were sea cadets who had been aboard the freighter *Elsass* which on the night before war was declared had raced out of Sydney Harbour only to be later interned at Pago Pago. The cadets had been among those sailors from the freighter who had escaped in a boat and rowed to Apia in the belief that the *Scharnhorst* and the *Gneisenau* had reinstated German authority there, only to find for their pains that they escaped the relative comfort of internment under the Americans to find themselves in the hands of the New Zealanders who promptly put them into a prisoner-of-war camp. Von Luckner chose one other man for his escape crew: Albrecht von Egidy, a former plantation owner in German Samoa and now an internee.

The commander of the prison camp, Lt. Col. Charles Harcourt Turner, who had been officer commanding, the 5th (Wellington) Regiment, for the 1914 occupation of German Samoa, had two methods of communicating with the mainland in an emergency; by telephone or by use of a fast motorboat called the *Pearl*. Curiosity to see the captured Germans had brought the New Zealand Minister of Defence, Sir James Allen, to visit Motuihe and he noticed that the guards did not seem to be armed, which, as he later reported, had struck him as odd at the time.

Access to the launch was not a problem for the Germans. Two of the prisoners were engineers and so had made themselves useful by giving *Pearl* a complete overhaul. The official inquiry which followed the escape now being planned by von Luckner was told that one German had worked regularly as an engineer on the *Pearl*, the other as a deck hand. They were given the task of returning the launch to its moorings after use, as the dinghy which served as a tender could take only two men. During the overhaul the German engineers had managed to secure a cache of spares by claiming that more parts needed replacement than was in fact the case. Trials were held to find how the *Pearl* handled in the open sea, and von Luckner thus determined that about three tonnes of stores would give her sufficient stability. Meanwhile, other men were using the camp workshops to make compasses and other nautical instruments.

Before the daring escape: Von Luckner (centre) and Leutnant Carl Kircheiss (right) out for a seemingly relaxed stroll with a New Zealand camp official. [Frederick Stunzer]

The New Zealand guard — by the time the Germans escaped, the guards were working unarmed. [Frederick Stunzer]

A sextant was fashioned from an old steering wheel which was cut in half to form the base. Properly made sextants could be obtained for a few pounds in Auckland, and while von Luckner appeared to have had adequate supplies of New Zealand money, no opportunity arose for him to get across to the city. They had a good map of Waitemata Harbour and the surrounding area, which they had copied from the one carried in the *Pearl*. Other maps were taken from atlases in the prison library, which Kircheiss copied and enlarged. These would do until they captured a ship with proper charts. A track was kept of all troop and guard movements by tapping the telephone wires.

The Germans had stolen the commandant's sword from the orderly room when it was clear that the guards were starting to become slack in their patrols. The guards had stopped carrying their rifles and walked about armed only with canes and whistles; later this was explained to the inquiry as being necessary as an economy measure! Anything else that was needed for the escape would be obtained by the simple stratagem of adding items to the requisition list for the launch after it had been signed by the commandant.

It was now December 1917 and von Luckner claimed he was aware that the *Wolf*, which he described as 'sister raider to the *Seeadler*' was off the north coast of New Zealand, and that if he could get a vessel with a wireless he would soon be able to communicate with the other raider. Nerger was, in fact, back in the Atlantic by this time. Von Luckner concluded: 'I felt certain that had the commander of the *Wolf* known that I was a prisoner on Motuihi Island he would have found some means of getting me away. I do not think that had anything to fear as regards coming into the harbour'.

Nevertheless, the preparations went on: some blasting explosives were found, a dummy machinegun was made and by 3 December each of the men chosen for the escape had their kit bags complete. Others who were sympathetic to the escapade agreed to keep watch for guards and to cut the telephone wire on the night.

They settled on 13 December. That afternoon the two German engineers aboard the *Pearl*, instead of returning the launch to its mooring after dropping off the staff who had arrived back from Auckland, steered her around to another part of the island where von Luckner's party was waiting. As soon as the escape became known to the commandant, he tried to telephone Auckland but the Germans had already cut the telephone line simply by earthing the wire.

Von Luckner headed up the Hauraki Gulf past Waiheke Island then made directly for Cape Colville, the northernmost tip of the

Coromandel Peninsula. By the next morning the Germans has passed the cape and were heading for the Mercury Islands where, in a quiet bay, repairs would be carried out to the launch's engine and a wireless aerial erected. Von Luckner had all along intended to make for the Kermadec Islands (which had proven so useful to Nerger, although von Luckner could not have known this) where there were provision depots for shipwrecked sailors, as he knew from his merchant experience in the Pacific. In the latter years of the nineteenth century the New Zealand Government, alarmed by the number of shipwrecks on its various island out-posts, had accordingly equipped them with castaway depots. In the case of the Kermadecs there were two, one on Curtis and one on Macauley Island. Strangely, Nerger had never found out about these. The depots on the Kermadecs consisted of a small iron shed, with spouting to capture rain water. They were equipped with biscuits, medicines, clothing and other necessary items. Von Luckner's plan was to capture a sea-going vessel, go to the islands and raid the stores, leave the crew of the captured vessel there, and then make for South America.

The Germans kept watch from a hill on the Mercury Islands for a likely victim. After a two-day wait, they saw two schooners coming up from the south. Von Luckner decided to attack the one lying astern, and the launch headed for it. Most of the Germans hid below while the New Zealand flag fluttered in the stiff breeze. He hailed the scow and her master brought his vessel into the wind and waited for the launch to catch up. She was the ninety tonne *Moa*, owned by the Leyland O'Brien Timber Company and engaged in the timber trade between Auckland and Tauranga. This day she was carrying 2,240 cubic metres of timber from Omokoroa on Tauranga Harbour. Despite her small size *Moa* was capable of making an ocean voyage. The crew consisted only of the master and four men. There was also an eleven year old boy aboard, the stepson of one of the crew, who was taking the voyage for his health.

The Moa. [Auckland Institute and Museum]

The skipper, Captain William Bourke, later recounted that von Luckner had come aboard followed by his armed party. He stated 'You are prisoners of war to Germany' and proceeded to haul up the German ensign. The crew, who were totally unarmed, were told they would have to continue to work ship and that they would be paid for their work.

The *Moa* was then turned about and set sail toward the Kermadecs, a course it held for five days until landfall. The Germans and New Zealanders shared the watches on the voyage.

On reaching the Kermadecs the scow was hove to; the *Pearl* had not survived the passage in tow and had sunk in bad weather after being swamped. She had gone down with the wireless set. About half the deck cargo of timber on *Moa* had been thrown overboard for the safety of the ship in the high seas, the lost sawn rimu being worth about £600.

After Bourke's initial outburst that it was 'damned hard luck to be caught this way', the two captains seem to have got along quite well. Von Luckner and Kircheiss installed themselves in Bourke's quarters aft, and the picture of Kitchener in the crew's mess was removed. The discipline among the Germans was rigid and, although they showed considerable animosity toward the British in general, this was not translated into personal antagonism toward the *Moa's* crew.

When the German lookout on Mercury Island had sighted the *Moa*, she had been trailing some eight kilometres behind another scow, the *Rangi*, which belonged to the Auckland firm of Winstone Ltd. The *Rangi* was travelling from Mayor Island, about thirty-five kilometres north of the *Moa's* point of origin. Her skipper, Captain Jack Francis, had seen the launch go alongside the other vessel and then shortly afterwards watched the *Moa* sail away in a different direction under press of canvas.

The *Rangi* thereupon altered course and headed for Port Charles on Coromandel Peninsula where Francis reported his suspicions to the postmaster. An hour later the government cable steamer, the *Iris*, was seen coming around Cape Colville and Francis took a boat and went out to her. The *Iris* had been equipped with two army six-pounders; with which she would subdue and capture the Germans, should the opportunity arise.

While Auckland's morning paper reflected the anger and humiliation which New Zealand was feeling at the Germans' successful escape, Lt. Col. Harcourt Turner was being relieved of his post as commandant at Motuihi, pending the outcome of an official inquiry.

On reaching the Kermadecs, von Luckner had decided to take all he could from the depot at Curtis Island, a bleak volcanic outcrop of fifty-one hectares. He would then land the *Moa*'s crew on Macauley Island where they could live off the castaway depot there until rescued.

What he did not count on was that the New Zealanders already had a shrewd idea where he was going. While the *Moa* was anchored off Curtis Island, with the dinghy away on its second trip to the stores depot, smoke appeared on the horizon.

The Germans swung in to action, raising sail as fast as they could to try to outrun the approaching ship. The chase lasted for an hour and a half when, at a range of more than 3,000 metres, *Iris* fired across the *Moa*'s bows. Von Luckner knew that the jig was up. He brought the scow head to wind and took in the headsails. As he stepped aboard the *Iris*, once more a prisoner-of-war of the New Zealand government, he said: 'You left the door open, you cannot blame me for walking out.'

The re-captured Germans were sent, after a short time in Auckland's Mt Eden gaol, to various camps around the country.

Von Luckner and Kircheiss were imprisoned on tiny Ripapa Island in Lyttelton Harbour in New Zealand's South Island. The war ended while von Luckner was planning yet another escape. The Germans were all repatriated in 1919.

In the mid-1930s Count Felix von Luckner revisited New Zealand where he was treated as an honoured guest; he was sailing around the world on his private yacht, the *Vaterland*. His reception was not so cordial when he called at Papeete — they still remembered the day in 1914 when the *Scharnhorst* and the *Gneisenau* had bombarded the town for twenty minutes.

Von Luckner lived in Germany during World War II and thereafter retired to western Sweden, where he died in 1966.

Postscript

BACK in 1996, Australian academic (and author of a doctoral thesis on the German East Asian Squadron) Peter Overlack pondered what effect von Spee's ships had on the conduct of the war. As he pointed out, even if the German cruisers could have maintained coal supplies, they could not replenish munitions and any more than two engagements would exhaust their firepower.

The squadron's unknown whereabouts in that first month of the war in 1914, though, did much to hamper the British over a wide area, he wrote in *The Journal of Military History*.

> Chartering came to a standstill, many of the regular lines cancelled their sailings in whole or part, and Middle Eastern and Far Eastern trade was reduced to a fraction of its normal volume. The restriction on banking facilities made it difficult to finance transactions and the Chinese ports were blocked by the accumulation of stock. As a result of these conditions, the freight markets of Shanghai, Yokohama and Manila were severely affected.

When the Emden was on the loose, the export of coal from Bengal came to a halt, too.

As for the squadron itself, it added a great deal of strain to the British empire's naval effort as the Royal Navy strained to meet the sudden burden of a huge war. A total of 102 vessels were diverted from other uses by the presence of the Germans in the Pacific if you count not only those searching for the enemy and patrolling the normal shipping routes but those now needed for convoy duty. And the need to prevent the German ships from using their South Pacific colonies for coaling was one factor that made it urgent for Australia and New Zealand to occupy New Guinea and Samoa respectively — but, as Overlack points out, that meant tying up troop transports that were needed to get Australasian soldiers to the European and Middle East theatres. And, of course, the occupation of the small island colonies in the Pacific also deprived von Spee of the radio network needed to operate effectively in the Pacific.

But he also raises the intriguing question of how different things might have been if the German squadron had been able to remain in the Pacific.

*   *   *

Germany was far better prepared for commerce raider warfare the next time around, in 1939, and the gentlemanly standards of 1914–18 had disappeared to a large extent. The Germans began planning for the use of auxiliary cruisers as early as 1936, with the initial aim of cutting North Africa off from France — thus preventing the flow of essential war materiel across the Mediterranean Sea. They had learnt the lesson of 1914: you simply cannot fit guns to a liner or merchantman and hope that it will be able to run amok in the ocean. Ships were chosen in advance, crews were trained for the specific task of manning the raiders.

Great attention was paid to disguise, so that in 1939 the raiders went forth with carpenters and other tradesmen aboard who could alter the ship's appearance overnight by changing the colours of the hull or erecting false funnels. The *Atlantis* was even supplied with Japanese women's clothing and prams so that its crew could stroll along the decks when the raider was posing as a Japanese liner.

The brutality during the World War II was far greater, not only because raiders would sometimes attack without warning, but it was also due to the refusal of most masters to give themselves up without some sort of resistance. Almost all the ships, when told to keep radio silence, immediately began sending either Q.Q.Q. signal ('Have been ordered to stop by an unidentified merchant-man') or R.R.R. ('Have been ordered to stop by surface raider') and stopped only after being fired upon. Several ships caught by the *Atlantis* (such as the *Scientist*, the *Tirrana*, and the *Automedon*) sustained severe damage and many casualties by trying to warn other Allied ships of the raider's presence.

These later raider captains could not boast, as von Luckner had done, that no one had died from their raiding activities. The *Atlantis* shelled a passenger liner after tracking her all night, without any attempt to warn or challenge the other vessel: the Egyptian liner *Zam Zam* had more than one hundred women and children aboard. Fifteen people died when the New Zealand Shipping Company liner *Rangitane* was sunk outward bound from Auckland.

The raiders of World War II sank a great many more ships than did their predecessors and, more importantly, sank a great many more bigger ships, which were losses felt more keenly by the Allied war effort.

As far as Australia was concerned, though, its gravest loss was the cruiser *Sydney*, sunk in the Indian Ocean in November 1941 with the loss of all lives after the mutually destructive action with the German raider *Kormoran*. That story has been told in full elsewhere, but it showed that the raiders of World War II were as deadly as any warship afloat having, as they did, the element of surprise.

The World War Two role call:

Orion: Captured/sank six ships, total tonnage 39,132.

Orion and *Komet* together: Captured/sank seven ships, total tonnage 43,162 (including Rangitane, 16,712 tons.

Komet (second cruise): Captured/sank three ships, total tonnage 21,738.

Atlantis: Captured/sank 22 ships, total tonnage 145,968.

Widder: Captured/sank ten ships, total tonnage 58,644.

Thor: Captured/sank 22 ships, total tonnage 152,134.

Pinguin: Captured/sank 28 ships, total tonnage 136,642.

Stier: Captured/sank four ships, total tonnage 30,728.

Kormoron: Captured/sank eleven ships, total tonnage 68,724 (including *Sydney*).

Michel: Captured/sank eighteen ships, total tonnage 127,018.

Appendix

Cruising Strength
in the Pacific, 1914

The French cruiser Montcalm *seen here in 1901, having been launched in 1900. She was equipped with two 195 mm and two 160 mm guns. She escorted the New Zealand force to Samoa and was a constant worry to the* Emden *whose commander had heard various rumours that* Montcalm *was chasing him. Had the French being doing so, and had caught the* Emden, *the* Montcalm *could have used her superior fire power to devastating effect.* [French Navy]

The following is a summary of cruising strength of the great powers in the Pacific at the outbreak of war in August 1914:

GERMANY
Scharnhorst and *Gneisenau* (Armoured cruisers) Built 1907-08
11,832 tons
Maximum speed: 22.5 knots
Complement: 765
Dimensions: 136m × 21m × 7.6m
Armament: Eight 210 mm, six 150 mm, twenty 24 pounders,
    four machine guns, four torpedo tubes.
Maximum fuel: 2,000 tonnes of coal.

Emden (Light cruiser) Built 1908
3,672 tons
Maximum speed: 24.5 knots
Complement 321
Dimensions: 117.6m × 13.1m × 5.3m
Armament: Ten 105 mm, eight 5-pounders, four machine guns,
    two torpedo tubes.
Maximum fuel: 900 tonnes of coal.

Nürnberg (Light cruiser) Built 1906
3,519 tons
Maximum speed: 23.5 knots Complement: 295
Dimensions: 107.6m × 13.5m × 5.3m
Armament: As for the *Emden*
Maximum fuel: 850 tonnes of coal.

Leipzig (Light cruiser) Built 1905
3,315 tons
Maximum speed: 23 knots
Complement: 286

Dimensions: 103.6m × 13.2m × 5.3m
Armament: As for the *Emden*
Maximum fuel: 800 tonnes of coal.

AUSTRALIA
Australia (Battle cruiser) Built 1912 (sister ship to *Indefatigable*)
19,580 tons
Maximum speed 25 knots
Complement: 800
Dimensions: 178.7m × 24m × 8.4m
Armament: Eight 305 mm, sixteen 100 mm, three torpedo tubes
Maximum fuel: 1,020 tonnes of coal.

Melbourne and *Sydney* (Light cruisers). Built 1913
5,700 tons
Maximum speed: 25.5 knots
Complement: 390
Dimensions: 139m × 15.2m × 5.4m
Armament: Eight 150 mm, two torpedo tubes.

Encounter (Light cruiser) Built 1902
5,900 tons
Maximum speed: 20 knots
Dimensions: 113m × 17m × 6.3m
Armament: Eleven 150 mm, eight 12-pounders, two torpedo tubes

Parramatta, Yarra, Warrego (River Class Torpedo-boat destroyers).
Parramatta and *Yarra* launched 1910, *Warrego* launched 1911.
700 tons
Maximum speed: 28 knots
Complement: 66
Dimensions: 76m × 8.2m × 3.3m
Armament: One 100 mm, three 12-pounders, three torpedo tubes.

Pioneer (Third class cruiser). Built 1899
2,177 tons
Maximum speed: 20.5 knots
Complement: 224
Dimensions: 95.4m × 11.2m × 5.1m
Armament: Eight 100 mm, eight 3-pounders, two torpedo tubes.

NEW ZEALAND

Philomel (Third class cruiser). Built 1890
2,625 tons
Maximum speed: 16.5 knots (19 'if pressed')
Complement: 217
Dimensions: 80.5m × 12.4m × 5.6m
Armament: Eight 120 mm, eight 3-pounders, two torpedo tubes.

Psyche, Pyramus
As for the *Pioneer* except *Pyramus* built 1898.

Other Forces:

BRITAIN

		Largest guns:	Top speed:
Triumph	Battleship.	255 mm	20 knots
Minotaur	Arm.Cruiser	235 mm	23 knots
Hampshire	Arm.Cruiser	190 mm	22 knots
Monmouth	Arm.Cruiser	150 mm	23 knots
Yarmouth	Lt. Cruiser	150 mm	25 knots
Newcastle	Lt. Cruiser	150 mm	25 knots
Glasgow	Lt. Cruiser	150 mm	25 knots

CANADIAN

Rainbow	3rd Cl. Cruiser.	150 mm	20 knots

AUSTRIAN

Kaiserin-Elisabeth	Old cruiser	150 mm	19 knots

JAPANESE

Hiyei	Battle-cruiser	355 mm	27.5 knots
Kongo	Battle-cruiser	355 mm	27.5 knots
Ibuki	Battle-cruiser	305 mm	22 knots
Kurama	Battle-cruiser	305 mm	21 knots
Ikoma	Arm. Cruiser	305 mm	20.5 knots
Tsukuba	Arm. Cruiser	305 mm	21 knots
Yakumo	Arm. Cruiser	205 mm	20 knots
Idzumo	Arm. Cruiser	205 mm	21 knots
Iwate	Arm. Cruiser	205 mm	21 knots
Adzuma	Arm. Cruiser	205 mm	21 knots
Asama	Arm. Cruiser	205 mm	21.5 knots
Tokiwa	Arm. Cruiser	205 mm	21.5 knots
Kasuga	Arm. Cruiser	255 mm	20 knots
Aso	Arm. Cruiser	205 mm	21 knots
Nisshin	Arm. Cruiser	205 mm	20 knots

Plus seven light cruisers with 150 mm armament, seven small cruisers with maximum armament ranging from 205 to 120mm and four gunboats.

RUSSIA

Zemtchug	Lt. Cruiser	120 mm	24 knots
Askold	Small Cruiser	150 mm	23 knots

Plus twenty destroyers and eight submarines stationed in the Pacific.

FRANCE

Montcalm	Arm. Cruiser	195 mm	21 knots
Dupleix	Arm. Cruiser	160 mm	21 knots

Plus two sloops.

Selected Bibliography

Journal articles

Andere, Phil, "The Real History of the Emden's Raid and Capture", *Zodiac*, Vol. VIII, No, 89, 1915.

Henderson, W. O. "Germany's Trade with her Colonies 1884-1914", *The Economic History Review*, Vol. IX, No 1, November 1938.

'Nakhoda', "The Cable Service in the War and the *Emden* Affair", *PFA Quarterly*, December 1921.

Overlack, Peter, "The Force of Circumstance: Graf Spee's Options for the East Asia Cruiser Squadron in 1914", *Journal of Military History*, 60:4, 1996.

Rentz, William Oliphant Kendrick, "The Confederate States Ship *Georgia*," *The Georgia Historical Quarterly*, Vol. 56, No. 3, Fall 1972.

Snow, Karen A., "Russian Commercial Shipping and Singapore, 1905-1916", *Journal of Southeast Asian Studies*, Vo. 29, No. 1, 1998.

Spinks, Charles Nelson, "Japan's Entrance in the World War", *Pacific Historical Review*, Vol. 5, No. 4, December 1936.

Treat, Payson J., "The Shantung Issue" *The Journal of International Relations*, Vol. 10, No. 3, January 1920.

Books

Alexander, Roy, *The Cruise of the Raider Wolf*, Angus & Robertson, Sydney 1939.

Barker, Dudley, *Prominent Edwardians*, Alien & Unwin, London 1969 (for a portrait of Fisher and his naval reforms).

Brown, William, Home is the Sailor, Hurst & Blackett, London 1940.

Buley, E.C., *Glorious Deeds of Australasians in the Great War*, Andrew Melrose, London 1915.

Burdick, Charles, *The Frustrated Raider- The Story of the German Cruiser Cormoran,* Southern Illinois University Press, Carbondale 1979.

Campbell, V.Adm. Gordon, *Sailormen All*, Hodder & Stoughton, London 1933.

Chatterton, E. Keble, *The Sea Raiders*, Hurst & Blackett, London 1931.

Davidson, J.W., *Samoa mo Samoa*, Oxford, Melbourne 1967.

Drew, Lt. H.T.B., *War Effort of New Zealand*, Whitcombe & Tombs, Christchurch 1923.

Dixon, Campbell, 'How the Emden Went to Her Doom' in Lewis, Leonard, *Epics of Empire,* Dean & Son, London.

Donaldson, Capt. A., *The Amazing Cruise of the German Raider Wolf*, NewxCentury Press, Sydney 1919.

——*Fifty Years Too Soon*, Whitcombe & Tombs, Melbourne 1948

Firth, Stewart, *New Guinea Under the Germans*, Melbourne University Press, Melbourne 1982.

Foreman, Amanda. *A World on Fire, an Epic History of Two Nations Divided.* Allen Lane, London, 2010.

Gartzke, Kapitanleutnant, 'The Rebellion of Ponape and its Suppression by HMS *Emden, Nurnberg, Cormoran, Planet*', in *Marine Rundschau*, Berlin 1911.

Godshall, W.L., *Tsingtao Under Three Flags*, Commercial Press, Shanghai 1929.

Hoehling, A.A., *Lonely Command*, Cassell, London 1957.

Hohne, Heinz, *Canaris*, Seeker & Warburg, London 1979.

Howard, M.G., 'New Zealand Naval Policy 1885-1921', unpub. thesis at Otago University, Dunedin 1954.

Hoyt, Edwin P., *Count von Luckner: Knight of the Sea*, David McKay, New York 1969.

——*The Last Cruise of the Emden*, Andre Deutsch, London 1967.

——*The Raider Wolf*, Arthur Barker, London 1974. (Hoyt has written prolifically on naval warfare, always with a racy narrative; in the above titles he relies heavily on accounts by German participants.)

Jose, A.W., *Royal Australian Navy*, Angus & Robertson, Sydney 1928 (A magisterial account of the war at sea 1914–18 from the Australian point of view.)

Joseph, Franz, Prince of Hohenzollern, *Emden*, Herbert Jenkins, London 1928.

Kennedy, P.M., *The Samoan Tangle*, University of Queensland Press, St Lucia 1974.

Langmaid, Capt. K., *The Sea Raiders*, Jarrolds, London 1963.

Le Sueur, Gordon, *Germany's Vanishing Colonies*, Everett & Co, London 1915.

Luckner, Felix von, *Pirate von Luckner and the Cruise of the Seeadler*, Godds and Bloomfield, Auckland 1919.

McGibbon, I.C., *Blue Water Rationale*, Department of Internal Affairs, Wellington 1981.

Mackenzie, S.S., *The Australians at Rabaul*, Angus & Robertson, Sydney 1927.

Miicke, Hellmuth von, *The Ayesha: A Good Adventure*, Phillip Alien & Co. London 1930.

——*The Emden*, Ritter & Co, Boston 1917.

Newbolt, Henry, *History of the Great War: Naval Operations*, Vol. IV, Longman Green, London 1928.

Paterson, A.B., *Happy Dispatches*, Angus & Robertson, Sydney 1935.

Plowman, Peter, *Passenger Ships of Australia and New Zealand*, Vols. I and 11, Doubleday, Sydney 1981.

Reeves, Signaller L.C., *Australians in Action in New Guinea*, Australasian News Company, Sydney 1915.

Schofield, Guy H., *The Pacific: Its Past and Its Future*, John Murray, London 1919.

Schuler, P.F.E., *Australia in Arms*, J. Fisher Unwin, London 1916.

Scott, Ernest, *Australia During the War*, Angus & Robertson, Sydney 1936.

Simpson, Colin. *The Ship that Hunted Itself*, Penguin 1979.

Schmalenbach, Paul. *German Raiders, A history of auxiliary cruisers of the German Navy 1895-1945*, Patrick Stephens, Cambridge, 1979

Staniforth Smith, Lt., the Hon., *Australian Campaigns in the Great War*, Macmillan, London 1919.

Taylor, A.J.P., *Germany's First Bid for Colonies*, Macmillan, London 1938.

Thomas, Lowell, *Lauterbach of the China Sea*, Hutchinson, London.

Van der Vat, Dan., *The Last Corsair*, Hodder & Stoughton, London 1983.

Waters, S.D., *The Royal New Zealand Navy*, Department of Internal Affairs, Wellington 1956.
Watson, R.M., *History of Samoa*, Whitcombe & Tombs, Wellington 1918.
White, L.G.W., *Ships, Coolies and Rice*, Sampson, Law, Manston & Co, London 1936.